Goose berry Patch co.

Speedy
SUPPERS

A Country Store In Your Mailbox®

Gooseberry Patch
600 London Road
P.O. Box 190
Delaware, OH 43015

www.gooseberrypatch.com
1·800·854·6673

Copyright 2006, Gooseberry Patch 1-931890-76-5
First Printing, November 2006

Do you have a tried & true recipe...
tip, craft or memory that you'd like to see featured in a
Gooseberry Patch book? Visit our website at
www.gooseberrypatch.com, register and follow the easy steps
to submit your favorite family recipe.
Or send them to us at:

Gooseberry Patch
Attn: Book Dept.
P.O. Box 190
Delaware, OH 43015

Don't forget to include the number of servings your recipe makes,
plus your name, street address, phone number and e-mail
address. If we select your recipe, your name will appear right
along with it...and you'll receive a **FREE** copy of the book!

CONTENTS

Dedication

For everyone who loves terrifically tasty food...in no time!

Appreciation

Special thanks to all our friends who shared their super-speedy recipes...we thank you!

Breakfast for DINNER

Country Brunch Skillet

Coleen Lambert
Casco, WI

Bacon, potatoes and cheese combine to make a scrumptious meal!

6 slices bacon	1 t. salt
6 c. frozen diced potatoes	1/4 t. pepper
3/4 c. green pepper, chopped	6 eggs
1/2 c. onion, chopped	1/2 c. shredded Cheddar cheese

In a large skillet over medium heat, cook bacon until crisp. Remove bacon; crumble and set aside. Drain skillet, reserving 2 tablespoons drippings in skillet. Add vegetables, salt and pepper to drippings; cook and stir over medium heat for 2 minutes. Cover and cook, stirring occasionally, until potatoes are tender and golden, about 15 minutes. Make 6 wells in potato mixture; break one egg into each. Cover and cook over low heat for 8 to 10 minutes, until eggs are completely set. Sprinkle with bacon and cheese. Makes 6 servings.

Check an egg for freshness in a snap! Place an egg into a pan of cool salted water. If it sinks to the bottom, it's fresh. If it rises to the surface, time to toss it.

Breakfast for DINNER

Tex-Mex Scramble

Kathy Grashoff
Fort Wayne, IN

A flavorful mix of ingredients...sure to please!

2 t. oil
3 6-inch corn tortillas,
   cut into strips
1 onion, chopped

8 eggs, beaten
1 c. salsa
1/4 c. sour cream
2 green onions, chopped

Heat oil in a skillet; add tortilla strips and onion. Cook over medium heat until tortillas are crisp; pour eggs over the top. Cook over low heat for 4 to 5 minutes, or until eggs are cooked through. Top each serving with salsa, sour cream and green onions. Serves 4.

Club soda will shine up stainless steel sinks in a jiffy!
Use a cloth dampened with soda and rub sink
until stains disappear.

Strawberry Cheesecake French Toast

Kris Coburn
Dansville, NY

*I like to dress up this dish by topping it with extra powdered sugar,
fresh fruit and a drizzle of maple syrup.*

3-oz. pkg. cream cheese,
   softened
2 T. powdered sugar
2 T. strawberry preserves
8 slices country white bread

2 eggs
1/2 c. half-and-half
2 T. sugar
4 T. butter, divided

Combine cream cheese and powdered sugar in a small bowl; mix well.
Stir in preserves. Spread cream cheese mixture equally over 4 slices
of bread; top with remaining slices to form sandwiches. Whisk eggs,
half-and-half and sugar together in a medium bowl; set aside. Melt
2 tablespoons butter in a large skillet over medium heat. Dip each
sandwich into egg mixture, completely covering both sides. Cook
2 sandwiches at a time for one to 2 minutes per side, or until golden.
Melt remaining butter and cook remaining sandwiches as instructed
above. Slice diagonally and serve. Serves 4.

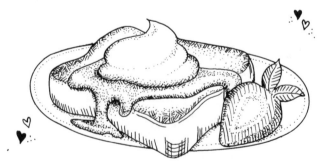

French toast is scrumptious topped with homemade whipped
cream. For the fluffiest whipped cream possible, always make
sure the bowl and beaters are chilled.

Mother's Cinnamon Cake

Vicki Channer
Fairview Heights, IL

My mother always made this recipe for our family, and still, the scent of cinnamon reminds me of this delicious recipe.

3/4 c. sugar
1/4 c. shortening
1 egg
1/2 c. milk
1 t. vanilla extract
1 c. all-purpose flour

1-1/2 t. baking powder
1/4 t. salt
1 T. butter, softened
3 T. powdered sugar
1 t. cinnamon

Gradually add sugar to shortening, blending until fluffy. Add egg; beat well. Stir in milk and vanilla; set aside. Mix together flour, baking powder and salt; stir into sugar mixture. Spread in a greased 9" round cake pan or 8"x8" baking pan. Bake at 375 degrees for 20 to 25 minutes. Remove from oven; immediately spread with butter. Mix together sugar and cinnamon; sprinkle over top. Serve warm. Makes 6 to 8 servings.

When brown sugar becomes hard, simply grate the amount needed in a recipe...a quick fix!

Onion Frittata

Linda Behling
Cecil, PA

My mother and grandmother used to make this dish throughout the spring and summer and it's a tradition that I continued to follow with my own children.

3 T. olive oil
1 T. butter
1-3/4 c. onion, thinly sliced

8 eggs
salt to taste

Heat olive oil and butter in a non-stick skillet. Add onion and sauté over medium-low heat just until golden and tender. Add a little water if onion gets too dry; remove to small bowl and set aside. Beat together eggs and salt; stir into onion mixture. Pour egg mixture into skillet; cook over low heat just until golden. Turn over and cook other side until golden. Cut into wedges; serve warm or at room temperature. Serves 4 to 6.

You'll shed fewer tears if you peel an onion under
cold running water. Try cutting the root end
off the onion last...that will help too!

Breakfast for Dinner

Egg-cellent Casserole

Julie Grau
McKinney, TX

This will bring everyone to the table!

1 lb. ground pork sausage,
   browned and drained
10-3/4 oz. can cream of
   mushroom soup

16-oz. pkg. shredded sharp
   Cheddar cheese
1 doz. eggs, scrambled

Mix all ingredients together; pour into a greased 13"x9" baking pan. Bake at 350 degrees for 20 to 25 minutes, or until eggs are set. Serves 6 to 8.

Ham & Feta Cheese Omelet

Holly Jackson
Saint George, UT

All I can say is "Mmm!"

2 eggs, beaten
1/4 c. feta cheese, crumbled
1/4 c. cucumber, diced
2 T. green onion, chopped

1/4 c. cooked ham, cubed
salt and pepper to taste
Garnish: salsa

Combine all ingredients except salsa in a bowl; mix well. Pour into a lightly greased skillet; cook over low heat until set. Fold over; transfer to serving plate. Serve with salsa. Makes one serving.

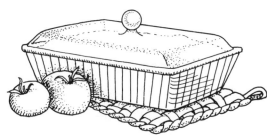

Make your fine china sparkle! Rinse it in a solution of 1/2 cup borax and warm water. Rinse well with clear water, then dry.

Beefy Potato Cakes

Zoe Bennett
Columbia, SC

*Make it fast…use leftover roast beef and mashed potatoes
from Sunday dinner!*

1 T. oil
1 onion, chopped
2 c. mashed potatoes

1 c. roast beef, shredded
salt and pepper to taste

Heat oil in a large skillet over medium heat; add onion and cook until tender. Transfer onion to a medium bowl; mix with potatoes, beef, salt and pepper. Form into 8 patties; return to skillet and cook over medium-high heat until golden on both sides. Makes 8 servings.

Mom's Texas Hash

Ginger O'Connell
Hazel Park, MI

Simply said…this is good!

1 lb. ground beef
2 onions, sliced
1 green pepper, chopped

8-oz. can stewed tomatoes
1/2 t. to 1 t. chili powder
1 t. salt

Brown beef, onions and green pepper in a skillet; drain. Stir in remaining ingredients. Cook over medium heat until heated through, about 8 minutes; spoon into an ungreased one-quart casserole dish. Bake at 350 degrees for 15 to 20 minutes. Serves 4.

For breakfast in a dash, pick up packages of heat & serve hashbrowns…real time-savers on busy days.

Breakfast for DINNER

Golden Home Fries

Jennifer Patrick
Gooseberry Patch

The ideal side dish for any main...eggs, quiche, pancakes. You can't miss when you pair up with these home fries.

3 T. olive oil, divided
1 onion, chopped
1 green pepper, chopped
4 redskin potatoes, cooked and
    cut into 1/2-inch cubes

3/4 t. paprika
1 t. salt
1/4 t. pepper
1/4 c. fresh parsley, chopped

Heat one tablespoon oil in a large skillet over medium heat. Add onion and green pepper; cook and stir until tender, about 5 minutes. Remove vegetables with a slotted spoon to a small bowl; set aside. Add remaining oil to skillet; increase heat to medium-high. Add potatoes, paprika, salt and pepper; cook and stir until golden, about 10 minutes. Stir in onion mixture and parsley; cook and stir for one additional minute. Serves 4.

Ranch House Burritos

Jason Keller
Carrollton, GA

Ring the dinner bell...they'll run to the table for these!

1 lb. ground pork sausage
1 green pepper, chopped
1 onion, diced
6 eggs, beaten

8 10-inch flour tortillas,
    warmed
Garnish: picante sauce

Combine sausage, green pepper and onion in a skillet over medium heat; cook until sausage is browned and vegetables are tender. Drain. Stir in eggs; cook until eggs are cooked through. Spoon mixture evenly into tortillas; roll up. Garnish with picante sauce. Serves 8.

Southern-Style Biscuits & Gravy

Darrell Lawry
Kissimmee, FL

Everyone's favorite...a must-have recipe!

1 lb. ground pork sausage
1/2 c. all-purpose flour
2 c. milk

salt and pepper to taste
12-oz. tube refrigerated biscuits,
    baked and split

Brown sausage in a large skillet over medium heat; drain. Add flour; cook for about one minute, or until flour is lightly golden. Add milk slowly, stirring constantly until thickened. Sprinkle with salt and pepper. Serve over split biscuits. Makes 4 servings.

Old-Fashioned Creamed Eggs

Melissa Grohman
York, PA

My sister-in-law passed this recipe from her family to ours.

1/4 c. butter
1/4 c. all-purpose flour
2 c. milk

6 eggs, hard-boiled, peeled
    and diced
salt and pepper to taste

Melt butter in a saucepan; stir in flour and milk. Cook and stir over medium heat until thickened. Fold in eggs; sprinkle with salt and pepper. Serves 3.

Did you know that sausage links will shrink less if they're lightly coated with flour before frying?

Breakfast for Dinner

Haystack Eggs

Melissa Cassulis
Bridgewater, NY

This is one of my dad's favorite breakfast treats. Mom has been making it for him for almost as long as I can remember!

1-3/4 oz. can shoestring
   potatoes
4 eggs

1 c. shredded Cheddar cheese
6 slices bacon, cooked and
   crisply crumbled

Spread potatoes evenly over the bottom of a greased 9" pie plate. Make 4 indentations in potatoes almost to bottom of pie plate. Carefully break one egg into each indentation. Bake at 350 degrees for 8 to 10 minutes, until eggs are almost set. Sprinkle with cheese and bacon. Return to oven; bake for an additional 2 to 4 minutes, or until eggs are set and cheese melts. Cut into 4 wedges; serve immediately. Makes 4 servings.

To keep the salt shaking, add 5 to 10 grains of rice inside the shaker. You can even wrap the shaker tightly with aluminum foil...the foil is moisture-proof and will keep the dampness out.

Ham, Mushroom & Bacon Quiche

Kaitlyn Kiser
Plainwell, MI

I've also substituted spinach and sausage or potatoes and broccoli for the ham, mushrooms and bacon. It's fun to experiment with lots of different ingredient combinations!

6 eggs, beaten
3/4 c. milk
salt and pepper to taste
1 c. shredded Cheddar cheese
2 to 3 slices bacon, crisply
    cooked and crumbled

4 slices deli ham, chopped
4-oz. can sliced mushrooms,
    drained
9-inch pie crust

Mix together eggs and milk in a medium bowl. Add salt and pepper; set aside. Sprinkle cheese, bacon, ham and mushrooms on top of crust; pour egg mixture over top. Bake at 350 degrees for 25 to 30 minutes, or until a toothpick comes out clean and top is golden. Serves 4.

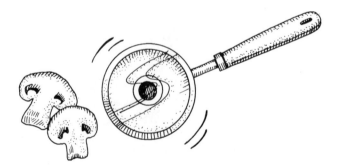

A pizza cutter is ideal for dividing up slices of quiche
while it's still in the pie plate.

Simply Scrumptious Frittata

Jill Valentine
Jackson, TN

A tasty way to use any remaining ham from Sunday dinner...try different cheeses for variety.

1 T. oil
1/2 c. onion, chopped
1/2 c. green pepper, chopped
1 to 2 cloves garlic, minced
4 potatoes, peeled, cubed
   and cooked

3/4 c. cooked ham, cubed
8 eggs, beaten
salt and pepper to taste
3/4 c. shredded Cheddar cheese

Heat oil in a heavy oven-proof skillet over medium heat. Add onion and green pepper; cook and stir until tender. Add garlic; cook for an additional minute. Stir in potatoes and ham; cook until heated through. Reduce heat to medium-low; add eggs, salt and pepper. Cook until eggs are firm on the bottom, about 5 minutes. Top with cheese; place in oven at 350 degrees for 5 to 10 minutes, or until cheese melts. Cut into wedges. Serves 4.

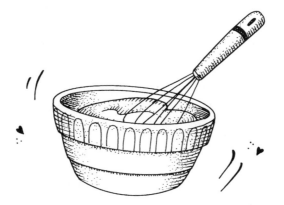

Remember that eggs will beat up fluffier for this frittata if they're at room temperature and not too cold.

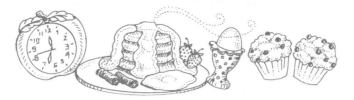

Cheesy Sausage Bake

Karen Carnes
Hartselle, AL

Two kinds of cheese make this casserole irresistible!

8-oz. tube refrigerated crescent
   rolls
1 lb. ground pork sausage,
   browned and drained
1 c. shredded Cheddar cheese

1 c. shredded mozzarella cheese
5 eggs
3/4 c. milk
salt and pepper to taste

Spread crescents in the bottom of a greased 13"x9" baking pan;
press together. Top with sausage. Sprinkle with cheeses; set aside.
Beat eggs, milk, salt and pepper together; pour over cheeses. Bake at
350 degrees for 25 minutes. Serves 6 to 8.

Crustless Zucchini Pie

Holly Sutton
Grahamsville, NY

This serves a lot, making it ideal for potlucks or carry-ins.

1 onion, chopped
1/2 c. oil
1/2 c. grated Parmesan cheese
4 eggs, beaten

1 T. fresh parsley, chopped
3 c. zucchini, grated
1 c. biscuit baking mix
1 c. shredded Cheddar cheese

Combine first 5 ingredients; mix well. Stir in remaining ingredients.
Pour into 2 greased 9" pie plates. Bake at 350 degrees for 25 to
30 minutes, until golden. Serves 8 to 10.

Blend equal parts olive oil and lemon
juice to create a polish that will make
wood furniture shine! Just apply
with a soft cloth and buff.

Breakfast for DINNER

Country-Style Supper Skillet

Rita Morgan
Pueblo, CO

Eggs, fresh tomatoes, bacon and potatoes combine to make this hearty dish one recipe you'll make again & again.

1/2 lb. bacon, chopped
3 potatoes, peeled, cooked
    and diced
1 c. tomato, chopped
1/2 c. onion, chopped
1/2 c. green pepper, chopped

1 t. garlic, chopped
salt and pepper to taste
1-1/2 c. shredded Cheddar
    cheese
8 eggs

Cook bacon over medium heat in a large deep skillet until crisp; partially drain drippings. Add vegetables, garlic, salt and pepper; sauté until tender, about 5 minutes. Sprinkle with cheese; crack eggs into skillet about 2 inches apart. Reduce heat; cover and cook eggs to desired doneness. Makes 4 to 6 servings.

If pots & pans become scorched during cooking, sprinkle them with baking soda. Add just enough water to moisten the baking soda and let stand overnight. Voilà! In the morning the scorched portion should lift right out.

Maple French Toast

Dawn Dhooghe
Concord, NC

Real maple syrup makes all the difference in this recipe!

3 eggs
1/2 c. maple syrup
1 c. milk
1/4 c. half-and-half
1/8 t. nutmeg

1/8 t. cinnamon
1/8 t. salt
6 to 8 slices bread
1 to 2 T. butter
Garnish: maple syrup

Whisk together eggs and syrup. Add milk, half-and-half, spices and salt; whisk until well combined. Dip bread into mixture, one slice at a time, turning to coat both sides. Melt butter in a skillet over medium heat; cook slices on both sides until golden. Serve with warm maple syrup. Serves 3 to 4.

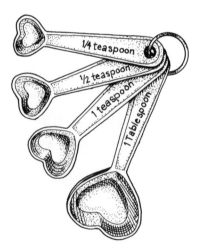

Before measuring sticky ingredients like syrup or honey, lightly oil the measuring cup, then rinse in hot water.

Breakfast for DINNER

Scrumptious Blueberry Pancakes

Jo Ann

Keep pancakes warm & toasty in an oven at 200 degrees.

1 c. milk
1/2 c. water
1 c. whole-wheat flour
1/2 c. cornmeal
1 t. baking powder

1/2 t. baking soda
1/4 t. salt
1 c. blueberries
2 T. oil, divided
Garnish: jam or syrup

Mix together milk and water in a small bowl; set aside. Sift together flour, cornmeal, baking powder, baking soda and salt in a large bowl; mix well. Stir in milk mixture just until combined. Fold in blueberries; let stand for 5 minutes. Heat one tablespoon oil in a large skillet over medium heat. Pour 1/4 cup batter per pancake onto hot griddle; cook until bubbly on top and edges are slightly dry. Turn and cook on other side until golden. Repeat with remaining oil and batter. Serve warm with jam or syrup. Makes one dozen pancakes.

A cup of herbal tea is perfect with breakfast recipes.
Instead of sweetening a cup of tea with sugar,
drop in one or 2 old-fashioned lemon drops.

Homestyle Corned Beef Hash

Athena Colegrove
Big Springs, TX

Use corned beef or roast beef for this quick & easy meal. Add a salad and rolls too...you'll find the whole family will enjoy it.

6 potatoes, peeled and diced
1 onion, chopped

12-oz. can corned beef, cubed
1 c. beef broth

Combine all ingredients in a large deep skillet over medium heat. Cover and simmer until potatoes are very tender and liquid is almost evaporated, about 20 to 25 minutes. Stir well before serving. Makes 4 to 6 servings.

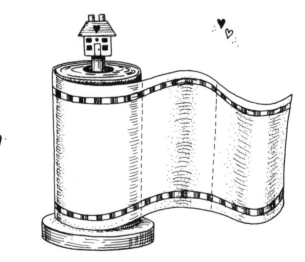

Brighten a white porcelain sink by placing paper towels across the bottom of the sink and saturating with bleach. Let sit overnight and rinse in the morning.

Breakfast for DINNER

Sausage & Rice & Everything Nice

Jackie Daunce
Lockport, NY

One Friday before grocery shopping day, I created this recipe on a whim with what was in the pantry. The kids loved it and now they ask me to make it all the time. They named it...Sausage & Rice & Everything Nice!

1-lb. pkg. mild Italian sausage links	14-1/2 oz. can diced tomatoes
6.8-oz. pkg. Spanish rice mix	4 eggs
	1/2 c. milk

Brown sausage in a large skillet over medium heat; cook until sausage is no longer pink, about 15 to 20 minutes. Drain; remove sausage from skillet, slice and set aside. Prepare rice, adding tomatoes, according to package directions; set aside. Whisk eggs and milk together. Add to skillet and cook over medium heat to desired doneness. Add sausage slices and rice to eggs; mix well. Serves 4 to 5.

Keep bread fresher longer...add a stalk of celery to the bread bag!

Hashbrown-Bacon Pie

Gladys Kielar
Perrysburg, OH

Our staff celebrates birthdays each month with a breakfast potluck...this is my favorite dish to share.

5 eggs
1/2 c. milk
3 c. frozen shredded
   hashbrowns, thawed
1/3 c. green onion, thinly sliced

1/2 t. salt
1-1/2 c. shredded sharp
   Cheddar cheese, divided
4 slices bacon, crisply cooked,
   crumbled and divided

Blend together eggs and milk; stir in hashbrowns, onion and salt. Add one cup cheese and half of the bacon. Pour into a greased 9" pie plate. Bake at 350 degrees for 25 to 30 minutes, until center is set. Sprinkle with remaining bacon and cheese; bake an additional 5 minutes. Cut into wedges. Serves 6.

Pepperoni & Cheese Quiche

Cheryl Lagler
Zionsville, PA

This quiche freezes well so I always prepare an extra one to freeze and enjoy later.

1 egg, beaten
3/4 c. all-purpose flour
1 c. milk
1/2 t. dried oregano
1/8 t. pepper

1/2 t. salt
1/2 c. Muenster cheese,
   shredded
1/2 c. shredded Cheddar cheese
1/4 c. pepperoni, finely chopped

Whisk together first 6 ingredients. Stir in cheeses and pepperoni. Pour into an ungreased 8" pie plate; bake at 375 degrees for 30 minutes, or until puffy and golden. Serves 4.

Garden-Fresh Griddle Cakes

Kim Ashby
Sinking Spring, PA

Zucchini and onion combine to make these savory griddle cakes.

2 c. zucchini, grated
2 eggs, beaten
1/4 c. onion, chopped
1/2 c. all-purpose flour
1/8 t. baking powder

1/4 t. dried oregano
oil for frying
Garnish: grated Parmesan
  cheese

Place zucchini in a colander; press to drain liquid. Transfer to a bowl. Mix in eggs and onion; set aside. Combine flour, baking powder and oregano; stir into zucchini mixture. Heat oil in a heavy skillet over medium heat. Drop batter by tablespoonfuls into hot oil; cook until golden. Sprinkle with Parmesan cheese. Serves 4.

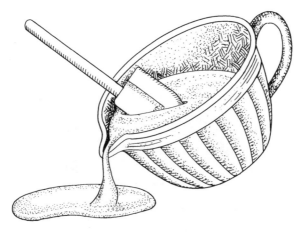

Fiberglass surfaces will shine when you wipe them down with a damp sponge sprinkled with borax!

Pumpkin-Maple Pancakes

Lora Montgomery
Gooseberry Patch

Serve with a dollop of whipped cream and a sprinkle of cinnamon.

2 c. all-purpose flour
2 T. brown sugar, packed
1 T. baking powder
1 t. salt
1 t. cinnamon
1/4 t. nutmeg

1/4 t. ground ginger
1-3/4 c. milk
1/2 c. canned pumpkin
1 egg
2 T. oil
Garnish: maple syrup

Stir together flour, brown sugar, baking powder, salt and spices in a medium bowl; set aside. Combine milk, pumpkin, egg and oil in a small bowl; mix well. Stir milk mixture into flour mixture just until blended. Heat a greased griddle over medium-high heat; pour batter onto griddle by 1/4 cupfuls. Cook until lightly golden on bottom and bubbles form on top; turn and cook other side until lightly golden. Serve with warm syrup. Makes 6 servings.

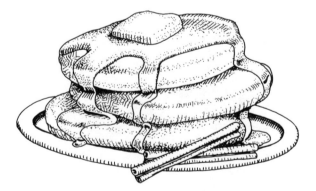

For speedy recipe prep, store all the breakfast foods on one shelf in the refrigerator and one shelf in your cupboard.

Peanut Butter French Toast

Flo Burtnett
Gage, OK

This is delicious! My grandson has been making this recipe for years and tops it with jam instead of syrup.

1/2 c. peanut butter	3/4 c. milk
12 slices bread, divided	1/4 t. salt
3 eggs	1/4 c. margarine

Spread peanut butter on 6 slices of bread; top with remaining bread. Blend together eggs, milk and salt; set aside. Dip each sandwich into egg mixture. Melt margarine in a skillet over medium heat; cook each sandwich until both sides are golden. Serves 6.

Lightly coat the inside of a cookie cutter with non-stick vegetable spray, then secure a clip-on clothespin to the side. Place in a skillet and add pancake batter inside the cookie cutter. Fun shaped pancakes and the clothespin makes it easy to remove the hot cookie cutter from the skillet.

Gingerbread Pancakes

Kathy Grashoff
Fort Wayne, IN

A yummy way to enjoy the flavor of gingerbread!

2-1/2 c. biscuit baking mix
3/4 c. apple butter
1 c. milk
2 eggs, beaten
2 T. oil

1/4 t. cinnamon
1/4 t. ground ginger
1/4 t. nutmeg
2 to 3 T. butter

Stir together all ingredients except butter until blended; set aside. Melt butter on a griddle or skillet over medium heat. Pour batter onto griddle by 1/4 cupfuls; cook until edges are done. Turn and cook until golden. Serves 6 to 8.

Sweet Coconut Toast

Hope Davenport
Portland, TX

Whenever I share this, everyone wants the recipe!

1 c. sweetened flaked coconut
1 c. sugar
1/2 c. butter, softened

1 egg, beaten
1 t. vanilla extract
11 slices white bread

Combine all ingredients except bread; mix well. Spread mixture on bread; arrange slices on an ungreased baking sheet. Bake at 350 degrees for 15 to 20 minutes, or until lightly golden. Serves 11.

Give boxed pancake mix a try when time is short. Add a sprinkle of cinnamon, sugar and a squeeze of lemon juice to the batter for real homemade taste.

Breakfast for DINNER

Quick-as-a-Wink Waffles

Laura Strausberger
Roswell, GA

Try these topped with jam or preserves, syrup or fresh fruit
and a dusting of powdered sugar.

2 eggs
3/4 c. milk
2 T. oil
1 c. all-purpose flour

1-1/2 t. baking powder
1-1/2 t. sugar
1/2 t. salt

Beat eggs until frothy in a medium bowl. Add remaining ingredients; mix until smooth. Pour by 1/2 cupfuls onto a preheated waffle iron; bake following manufacturer's directions. Serves 4.

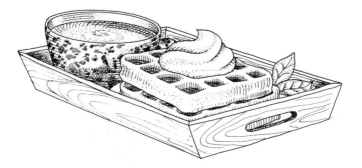

If part of a broken eggshell makes its way into your waffle or pancake batter, just dip a clean eggshell into the batter. The broken one will grab onto it like a magnet!

Happy-Happy Eggs

Kendra Harnden
Medicine Lodge, KS

How did this recipe get its name? Because they're quick-to-fix, Mom's happy and because they love to eat 'em, the kids are happy!

2 T. butter
2 c. frozen shredded
  hashbrowns
1 onion, chopped
1 red pepper, chopped
4-oz. can sliced mushrooms,
  drained

6 eggs
1/4 c. milk
1/4 t. pepper
1 lb. ground pork sausage,
  browned and drained
1/2 c. shredded Cheddar cheese

Melt butter in a large skillet over medium heat. Add hashbrowns, onion, red pepper and mushrooms. Sauté until tender; set aside. Whisk together eggs, milk and pepper; stir in sausage and pour over hashbrown mixture. Cover; cook over low heat until eggs are cooked through. Sprinkle cheese over top; heat until melted. Serves 4 to 6.

Best-Ever Brunch Casserole

Kim Baker
Bryan, TX

Make it a make-ahead casserole...just chill and bake the next day.

4 slices bread, torn
1 lb. ground pork sausage,
  browned and drained
6 eggs

1-1/2 c. milk
1 t. dry mustard
8-oz. pkg. shredded
  Cheddar cheese

Arrange bread in a greased 9"x9" baking pan. Sprinkle sausage over top; set aside. Whisk together eggs, milk and dry mustard; pour over sausage. Top with cheese; bake at 350 degrees for 25 to 30 minutes. Serves 4 to 6.

Classic Comfort FOOD

Homestyle Meatballs & Gravy

Tricia Wolfe
Richwood, OH

Delicious over buttered noodles or rice.

12-oz. pkg. frozen meatballs,
   thawed
12-oz. jar beef gravy

10-3/4 oz. can cream of
   mushroom soup
1 to 2 T. water

Arrange meatballs in a lightly greased 13"x9" baking pan; set aside.
Combine gravy, soup and water; pour evenly over meatballs. Bake
at 350 degrees for 20 to 25 minutes, or until heated through.
Serves 2 to 4.

Shepherd's Pie

Kathy Armstrong
Bayview, ID

Use your favorite cream soup or the one that's in the pantry!

1 lb. ground beef
1/2 c. onion, diced
10-3/4 oz. can cream of
   mushroom soup

1/4 c. plus 1 T. milk
1 c. green beans
3 c. mashed potatoes
1 c. shredded Cheddar cheese

Brown ground beef and onion in a large skillet over medium heat;
drain and return mixture to skillet. Add soup, milk and green beans to
skillet; mix well. Spoon ground beef mixture into a lightly greased
1-1/2 quart casserole dish. Spread potatoes on top of beef mixture and
sprinkle with cheese. Bake at 375 degrees for 20 to 25 minutes, or
until cheese is melted. Serves 4 to 6.

Dress up plain packages of
mashed potatoes with minced
garlic, chives or crumbled,
cooked bacon.

Classic Comfort FOOD

Chicken & Stuffing Bake

Sara Zimdars
Fredonia, WI

When Mom made dinner for my grandparents,
this was the quick & easy dish they loved!

1/2 c. water
1 T. margarine
4 c. herb-flavored stuffing mix
6 boneless, skinless chicken
    breasts, halved

1/8 t. paprika
10-3/4 oz. can cream of
    mushroom soup
1/3 c. milk
1 T. fresh parsley, chopped

Bring water and margarine to a boil in a large saucepan; remove from heat. Stir in stuffing mix. Spoon mixture across center of a lightly greased 3-quart casserole dish. Arrange chicken on each side of stuffing. Sprinkle with paprika; set aside. Combine soup, milk and parsley; pour over chicken. Bake, covered, at 350 degrees for 15 minutes. Uncover; bake for an additional 15 minutes, or until chicken is cooked through. Serves 6.

Did you know that plain club soda is an instant spot remover for fresh stains? It's wonderful! Pour a little on the spot, let set just a few seconds, then blot excess moisture.

Super-Easy Chicken & Noodles

Julie Thurman
Hamilton, OH

They'll think you worked in the kitchen all day!

1 lb. boneless, skinless chicken
    breast, cubed
1 T. oil
10-3/4 oz. can cream of
    chicken soup

1/2 c. milk
1/8 t. pepper
3 c. cooked medium egg noodles
1/3 c. grated Parmesan cheese

In a large skillet over medium heat, cook chicken in oil for 10 to
15 minutes, or until golden. Stir in remaining ingredients; heat
through. Makes 4 servings.

Creamy Beef & Onions

Rebecca Cook
Helotes, TX

Always a hit when I serve it over cooked rice or noodles.

1 lb. ground beef
1 onion, sliced
12-oz. jar beef gravy

1/4 c. sour cream
cooked rice or egg noodles

Brown beef and onion in a large skillet over medium heat; drain. Add
gravy and sour cream; heat through, about 5 to 10 minutes. Serve
over cooked rice or noodles. Serves 4.

You can save 30 minutes when roasting a turkey
if you roast it unstuffed! Try placing chopped carrots and leeks
under the turkey...the vegetables will flavor the drippings
and there's no rack to scour.

Classic Comfort FOOD

One-Pot Pork Chop Supper

Karen McCann
Marion, OH

A homestyle dinner that's oh-so tasty!

1 T. butter
4 boneless pork chops,
   1/2-inch thick
3 redskin potatoes, quartered
2 c. baby carrots

1 onion, quartered
10-3/4 oz. can cream of
   mushroom soup
1/4 c. water

Melt butter in a large skillet over medium heat. Add pork chops; sauté 3 minutes per side, or until golden. Add potatoes, carrots and onion. In a small bowl, combine soup and water; pour over pork chops. Cover and simmer for 15 to 20 minutes, or until vegetables are tender. Serves 4.

The glow of candlelight is so pretty...don't save candles for special occasions only! If the candleholders become coated with wax, simply place them in the freezer for a couple of hours and the wax will peel right off.

Buttery Garlic Mashed Potatoes

Mary Bettuchy
Chambersburg, PA

Kick up the flavor with even more garlic...if you dare!

6 potatoes, peeled and diced
1/2 c. butter, softened and
    divided

milk
4 cloves garlic, minced

Cover potatoes with water in a large saucepan. Bring to a boil; simmer until tender, about 15 to 20 minutes. Drain potatoes and return to saucepan. Mash slightly with a potato masher. Add half the butter; mash again. When butter melts, add a little milk and mash. Add remaining butter and garlic; mash until butter melts. Add milk as needed to bring to desired consistency; mash until smooth. Serves 6.

Try substituting frozen diced potatoes for fresh potatoes...just as tasty but without the work!

Classic Comfort Food

Creamy Macaroni & Cheese

Tricia Wolfe
Richwood, OH

Homemade mac & cheese couldn't be easier.

2 c. elbow macaroni, uncooked
1/4 lb. pasteurized process
    cheese spread, diced

salt and pepper to taste

Cook macaroni according to package directions; drain and return to pan. Stir in cheese; salt and pepper to taste. Serves 4.

If you've accidentally scorched a white cotton or linen tablecloth, dampen a cloth with peroxide, lay it over the scorched area and iron with a warm iron.

Chicken Tetrazzini

Susan Biffignani
Fenton, MO

A gourmet dinner in record time!

3 T. butter
1 onion, chopped
1/4 c. celery, chopped
2 c. cooked chicken, diced
10-3/4 oz. can cream of
    mushroom soup
2-1/2 c. chicken broth

1 t. lemon juice
1/4 t. pepper
1/8 t. nutmeg
6-oz. pkg. spaghetti, uncooked
    and coarsely broken
4-oz. can sliced mushrooms,
    drained

Heat butter in a large soup pot over medium heat. Sauté onion and celery in butter until tender; arrange chicken over the top. Stir in soup, broth, lemon juice, pepper and nutmeg; add spaghetti. Bring to a boil; reduce heat and simmer for 15 minutes, or until spaghetti is tender. Add mushrooms; simmer until mushrooms are heated through. Serves 8.

Paprika Chicken

Denise Erickson
Colorado Springs, CO

A crispy salad and some steamed veggies round out a super supper!

4 boneless, skinless chicken
    breasts
olive oil

1 onion, chopped
paprika to taste
1/2 c. water

Brown the chicken breasts in oil over medium heat. Add onion and sprinkle with paprika; pour in water. Cover; reduce heat and simmer until chicken is cooked through, about 15 minutes. Serves 4.

Classic Comfort FOOD

Topsy-Turvy Lasagna

Amy Blanchard
Royal Oak, MI

The fabulous flavors of lasagna, without the fuss!

3/4 lb. ground beef
28-oz. jar spaghetti sauce
5 c. cooked egg noodles

1 c. cottage cheese
8-oz. pkg. shredded mozzarella
cheese, divided

Brown ground beef in a skillet; drain. Stir in spaghetti sauce; simmer for 10 minutes. In a lightly greased 2-quart casserole dish, combine noodles, ground beef mixture, cottage cheese and one cup mozzarella cheese. Top with remaining mozzarella. Bake at 350 degrees for 15 to 20 minutes. Serves 6 to 8.

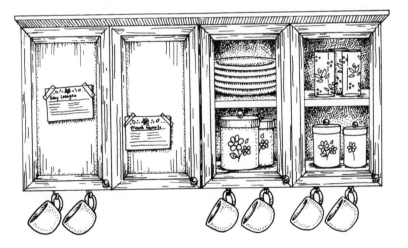

To reduce countertop clutter, tape recipes to cabinets
at eye level while cooking.

Cinnamon-Apple Muffins

Terri Childress
Staunton, VA

So nice with a steaming cup of herbal tea.

2 c. all-purpose flour, divided
1 c. brown sugar, packed
1/2 c. margarine, chilled and
　diced
1-1/2 t. baking powder
1/2 t. baking soda
1-1/2 t. cinnamon

1/2 t. salt
2/3 c. milk or buttermilk
1 egg, beaten
1 t. vanilla extract
2 apples, cored, peeled and
　finely chopped

Combine 1-1/3 cups flour, brown sugar and margarine in a large bowl. Mix with a pastry blender until mixture is consistency of fine crumbs; set aside 1/4 cup for topping. Add remaining flour, baking powder, baking soda, cinnamon and salt to same bowl; mix well. Slowly stir in milk or buttermilk, egg, vanilla and apples; stir just until moistened. Evenly divide batter among 16 greased muffin cups; sprinkle with reserved topping. Bake at 400 degrees for 20 to 24 minutes, or until a toothpick inserted in center comes out clean. Makes about 16.

Dab a drop of peppermint or lavender oil on a cool lightbulb. When you turn on the light, the scent will freshen any room.

Classic Comfort FOOD

Country Cornbread

DeNeane Deskins
Indian Harbor Beach, FL

Top individual slices with butter...there's nothing like it.

2 eggs
1-1/4 c. milk
1/4 c. shortening, melted and
   cooled

1-1/2 c. cornmeal
3/4 c. all-purpose flour
1 t. salt
2-1/2 t. baking powder

Beat eggs, milk and shortening together; set aside. Combine remaining ingredients; add to egg mixture. Pour into a greased 9"x9" pan; bake at 400 degrees for 20 to 25 minutes. Serves 6 to 8.

Don't forget to save any remaining cornbread to use in recipes for cornbread stuffing or cornbread salad.

Farm-Style Green Beans

Kerry Mayer
Dunham Springs, LA

Tastes like Grandma's homemade beans!

3 slices bacon, chopped
1/4 c. onion, chopped
15-oz. can green beans

1 cube chicken bouillon,
   crumbled

Cook bacon in a medium saucepan over medium heat. Add onion; cook for 5 minutes, or until onion is tender. Stir in green beans and bouillon. Bring to a boil; reduce heat and simmer for 15 minutes. Serves 4.

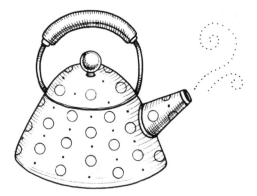

To remove the little dents in your carpet left by furniture, place ice cubes on the divots. The carpet fibers will swell as they absorb the water, then all you need to do is vacuum the carpet to pull up wet fibers.

Garlic Roasted Asparagus

Jeanne Calkins
Midland, MI

In just minutes you can whip up this savory side.

1 lb. asparagus, trimmed
1 T. olive oil

3 cloves garlic, pressed
salt and pepper to taste

Toss together all ingredients; arrange in a single layer on a lightly greased baking sheet. Bake at 450 degrees for about 8 to 12 minutes, until tender. Makes 4 servings.

To keep the kitchen sink tidy, shop flea markets for pretty trays to hold sponges, dish and hand soap. The trays will keep spills off the counter and make quick work of cleaning the sink.

Country-Fried Steak

Dana Thompson
Gooseberry Patch

Don't forget all the things that go with this...mashed potatoes, corn on the cob and rolls with butter.

1-1/2 c. all-purpose flour
1 t. paprika
1 t. salt
1/4 t. pepper
2 lbs. beef cube steak, cut into
    8 pieces

1 c. milk
1/4 c. oil
2.6-oz. pkg. country gravy mix,
    prepared

Combine flour, paprika, salt and pepper; set aside. Dip steak into milk, then into flour mixture, pressing to coat thoroughly. Heat oil in a large skillet over medium heat; add steak and cook 5 minutes on each side, or until golden and tender. Top with prepared gravy. Makes 8 servings.

To remove a gravy stain, sprinkle artificial sweetener or flour over the stained area to absorb the grease. Soak the tablecloth in a mixture of one teaspoon mild, colorless detergent for each cup of lukewarm water. Let sit 20 minutes, wash, then air dry.

Plantation Supper

Beth Garrison
Greenwood, IN

*This recipe is in memory of my Aunt Leah who made it
for us each time we visited her.*

1 lb. ground beef
1/2 c. onion, diced
1 c. frozen corn, cooked and
    drained
16-oz. pkg. frozen homestyle
    egg noodles, cooked
10-3/4 oz. can cream of
    mushroom soup

8-oz. pkg. cream cheese,
    softened
1/4 t. salt
1/4 t. pepper
1/2 t. garlic powder
1 to 1-1/2 t. chili powder

Brown ground beef with onion in a large pot over medium heat;
drain. Add cooked corn and noodles; mix well. Stir in remaining
ingredients and mix well. Cook over medium heat until heated
through, about 10 minutes. Serves 4 to 6.

Potatoes are a super side with any meal! Boil, bake or
microwave them with their skins on. Not only are they more
nutritious that way, but it saves a lot of preparation time!

Onion Glorified Pork Chops

Judy Kocian
Manitowoc, WI

Tender and delicious.

1 T. oil
6 pork chops
1 onion, sliced
1/2 t. dried thyme

10-3/4 oz. can cream of celery
   soup
1/4 c. water
Optional: cooked egg noodles

Heat oil in a large heavy skillet over medium-high heat; add pork chops. Cook until pork chops are browned on both sides, about 10 minutes. Remove from pan and set aside. Add onion and thyme to skillet; sauté over medium-low heat, stirring frequently, until onion is crisp-tender. Stir in soup and water; bring to a boil. Return pork chops to skillet, cover and cook over low heat for about 15 minutes. Serve over egg noodles if desired. Serves 6.

Give a homemade taste to packaged stuffing mixes with very little effort. Sauté 1/4 cup each of chopped onion and celery, add to the stuffing mix and prepare as the package directs.

Classic Comfort FOOD

Fried Potatoes, Green Beans & Bacon

Carolyn Erwin
Churubusco, IN

This is a simple skillet meal using only 4 ingredients.
Try it with diced ham too, you'll find it's also tasty.

1/2 lb. bacon
1/2 c. onion, sliced
4 potatoes, peeled and sliced

1-1/2 lbs. green beans, cooked
salt and pepper to taste

Cook bacon in a large skillet over medium heat until crisply cooked.
Remove bacon from skillet, reserving drippings; crumble bacon and set
aside. Add onion; cook until tender. Remove onion from skillet; set
aside. Add potatoes to remaining drippings; cook until fork-tender.
Drain skillet, leaving one tablespoon drippings in skillet. Add bacon,
onion, potatoes and cooked green beans to skillet; heat through.
Add salt and pepper to taste. Makes 4 servings.

Speed prep time as well as clean up time! Chop ingredients in
advance and place them in plastic cups. Store in the
refrigerator until needed later.

Mom's Comfort Casserole

Karen Tuinstra
Neshkoro, WI

There's just something special about Mom's cooking.

1 lb. ground beef
1/4 c. onion, chopped
salt and pepper to taste
10-3/4 oz. cream of mushroom
   soup

15-oz. can creamed corn
1 c. milk
16-oz. pkg. wide egg noodles,
   cooked

Brown ground beef and onion in a large skillet over medium heat; add salt and pepper to taste. Cook until beef is no longer pink; drain. Stir in soup, corn and milk; mix well. Simmer for about 10 minutes; add noodles, mixing well. Cover and simmer over low heat for an additional 10 minutes. Serves 4.

When stacking Grandma's china plates in the cupboard,
slip a paper plate between each to keep the china
from becoming scratched.

Classic Comfort FOOD

Sautéed Chicken & Onions

Mary Rita Schlagel
Warwick, NY

Ideal for Sunday dinner...easy to prepare, which leaves plenty of time for relaxing on the front porch.

4 T. all-purpose flour, divided
1 T. dried parsley
1/8 t. paprika
1/2 t. salt
1/8 t. pepper
4 boneless, skinless chicken breasts, halved

1/4 c. olive oil
4 onions, sliced
1 c. sliced mushrooms
1 c. chicken broth
1/2 c. white wine or chicken broth

Combine 2 tablespoons flour, parsley, paprika, salt and pepper in a plastic zipping bag; mix well. Place chicken in bag; shake to coat. Set aside. Heat oil in a skillet over medium heat; add chicken. Cook until chicken is golden on both sides and cooked through; transfer to a deep serving dish. Sauté onions and mushrooms over medium heat in skillet until tender; set aside. In a bowl, mix together broth and wine; stir in remaining flour. Add broth mixture to skillet; cook and stir until thickened. Pour over chicken. Serves 4 to 6.

Store clear plastic wrap in the refrigerator...it won't stick together when you need to use it!

49

Turkey Stroganoff

Lisa Ann Panzino-DiNunzio
Vineland, NJ

A true homestyle dish that's comfort food through and through.

1 lb. ground turkey
1/2 c. onion, chopped
1 clove garlic, finely chopped
10-3/4 oz. can cream of
    mushroom soup

4-oz. can mushroom stems and
    pieces, drained
1/2 t. salt
8-oz. container sour cream
cooked egg noodles or rice

Spray skillet with non-stick vegetable spray; heat over medium heat.
Add turkey, onion and garlic; cook 8 to 10 minutes, stirring occasionally, until turkey is no longer pink. Drain. Add soup, mushrooms
and salt. Simmer, uncovered, for about 10 minutes. Reduce heat to
low. Stir in sour cream; heat through. Serve over noodles or rice.
Makes 4 servings.

The best window cleaner is a snap to mix up. Fill a spray bottle
with 3 tablespoons ammonia, one tablespoon of vinegar
and fill with cool water. And to really make a window shine,
wipe it down with crumpled newspaper!

Classic Comfort FOOD

Cube Steak & Gravy

Cherylann Smith
Efland, NC

Just like Grandma's tried & true recipe.

1 to 2 T. oil
6 beef cube steaks
salt and pepper to taste

1 c. plus 1/4 c. all-purpose flour,
   divided
2 c. cold water

Heat oil in a large skillet over medium heat. Sprinkle steaks with salt and pepper; dredge in one cup flour. Add steaks to skillet. Cook until golden, turning 3 to 4 times to prevent sticking. Drain, reserving 2 tablespoons drippings; set aside. To make gravy, mix remaining flour with cold water until well blended. Add to skillet; cook over medium heat, stirring constantly, until thickened to desired consistency. If gravy is too thick, add water, one tablespoon at a time. Serve hot gravy with steaks. Makes 6 servings.

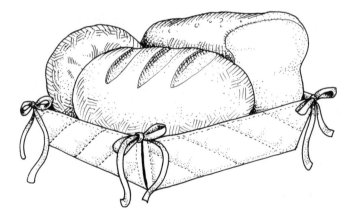

Buy loaves of savory bread at the market and then freeze them.
They will keep well and for dinner, just thaw and toast.

Skillet Cheese Bread

Margaret Collins
Wimauma, FL

Homemade bread in no time!

1/2 c. shortening, melted and
   cooled
2 eggs, beaten
1 c. milk
3 c. biscuit baking mix

8-oz. pkg. pasteurized process
   cheese spread, grated
2 T. poppy seed
2 t. dried, minced onion

Combine shortening, eggs, milk and biscuit mix; add remaining ingredients. Mix well; pour into a wax paper-lined cast iron skillet. Bake at 300 degrees for 20 minutes. Serves 12.

Mom's Sour Cream Biscuits

Jill Valentine
Jackson, TN

Oh-so simple to whip up.

2 c. all-purpose flour
1 t. salt

1/2 t. baking soda
1-1/4 c. sour cream

Sift together flour, salt and baking soda. Add enough sour cream to form a soft dough. Turn onto a floured board; knead slightly. Roll out 1/2-inch thick and cut with a floured round 2-1/2 inch cookie or biscuit cutter. Bake on a lightly greased baking sheet for 15 minutes at 500 degrees. Makes one dozen.

Scrumptious in seconds...top Skillet Cheese Bread or Mom's Sour Cream Biscuits with deli chicken, egg or ham salad. You can even top them with a fried egg, ham and cheese slice!

52

Roasted Dill Carrots

DeeAnne Manntz
Saginaw, MI

You can't miss with this side...goes with any main dish!

3 T. olive oil
1-1/4 t. kosher salt
1/2 t. pepper

12 carrots, peeled and sliced
diagonally 1-1/2 inches thick
2 T. fresh dill or parsley, minced

Combine oil, salt and pepper in a medium bowl; add carrots, coating well. Arrange carrots in a single layer on an ungreased baking sheet. Bake at 400 degrees for 20 minutes, until golden and tender. Toss carrots with dill or parsley. Serves 4 to 6.

Store your fresh parsley and cilantro in a paper towel
instead of the plastic bag from the grocery
and it will keep 3 times longer!

Baked Ziti Supreme

Jessica Parker
Mulvane, KS

Stop at the grocer's salad bar to mix up a family salad,
then choose a loaf of Texas toast to butter...yum!

1 lb. ground beef
1 onion, chopped
28-oz. jar spaghetti sauce with
   mushrooms

1-1/2 c. shredded mozzarella
   cheese, divided
5 c. cooked ziti pasta
1/4 c. grated Parmesan cheese

Cook beef and onion in a skillet over medium heat until beef is
browned; drain. Stir in spaghetti sauce, one cup mozzarella cheese and
ziti. Spoon into a lightly greased 3-quart casserole dish; sprinkle
with remaining mozzarella cheese and Parmesan cheese. Bake at
350 degrees for 25 to 30 minutes. Serves 6.

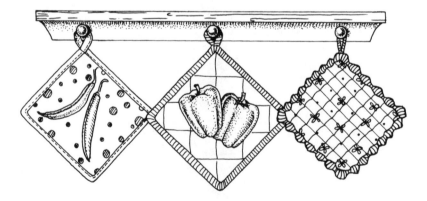

A speedy side...sauté frozen green beans until crisp-tender,
and toss with a jar of roasted red peppers.

Classic Comfort FOOD

Chicken Piccata

Cindy Watson
Gooseberry Patch

This recipe makes its own delicious sauce.
Try serving it with rice or pasta.

1/4 c. plus 2 T. all-purpose flour, divided
2 T. chicken bouillon granules, divided
4 boneless, skinless chicken breasts
2 T. olive oil

1 T. butter
1/2 c. white wine or chicken broth
1/4 c. lemon juice
2 T. water
2 T. capers, drained and rinsed
2 T. fresh parsley, chopped

Combine 1/4 cup flour and 1/2 teaspoon bouillon granules; set aside. Place chicken between 2 sheets of plastic wrap and pound to 1/4-inch thickness. Dip chicken in flour mixture to coat. Heat oil in large skillet over medium heat; cook chicken 4 to 5 minutes on each side, or until cooked through. Remove chicken and keep warm. Melt butter in skillet and add remaining flour, scraping up browned bits. Add wine or broth, lemon juice, water and remaining bouillon granules; simmer for 2 minutes. Stir in capers and parsley. Spoon sauce over chicken. Makes 4 servings.

Always keep the pantry stocked with canned vegetables, hearty soups, rice and pasta for quick-to-make side dishes.

My Mom's Cream Chicken

Erin Warfel
Nicholasville, KY

This recipe is a family favorite. Mom serves it on top of warm biscuits...delicious!

1/4 c. butter
1/4 c. plus 1 T. all-purpose flour
1 c. chicken broth
1 c. milk

1 egg yolk, beaten
2 c. cooked chicken, chopped
1/2 t. salt
pepper to taste

Melt butter in a large pan over medium heat; add flour, blending well. Gradually stir in broth, then milk. Reduce heat to low; cook until thickened, about 2 to 4 minutes, stirring constantly. Remove 1/4 cup milk mixture and gradually stir into egg yolk. Return egg mixture to milk mixture. Add chicken, salt and pepper; heat through. Serves 4 to 6.

1950's vintage metal chairs are springy and oh-so comfy. If they need a little face-lift, a good scrubbing with turpentine will remove rust.

Classic Comfort FOOD

Salisbury Steak

Karen McCann
Marion, OH

All I can say is this is delicious!

1 lb. ground beef
1/2 to 3/4 c. saltine crackers,
    crushed
1 egg, beaten
1/4 c. onion, chopped

1/2 t. salt
pepper to taste
1/2 c. water
10-1/2 oz. can brown gravy

Combine ground beef, cracker crumbs, egg, onion, salt and pepper in a large mixing bowl. Form into 6 to 8 patties; set aside. Combine water and gravy; pour into a large skillet over medium heat. Add patties. Cover and simmer for 25 to 30 minutes, turning halfway through. Serves 4 to 6.

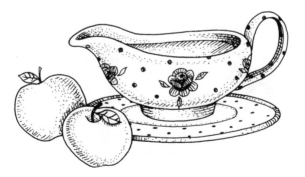

Kitchen-supply stores carry handy magnetic knife holders you can easily turn into oh-so clever paintbrush racks! Be sure to hang the brushes bristle-end down so they'll dry completely.

Grandma's Tomatoes

Peggy Donnally
Toledo, OH

This recipe brings back fond memories from my childhood.

28-oz. can diced tomatoes
3 T. butter, sliced
2 T. all-purpose flour
salt and pepper to taste

1/2 c. water
3 to 4 slices French or
    Italian bread, torn

Combine tomatoes and butter in a saucepan; cook over medium heat for 8 to 10 minutes. In a small bowl, combine flour, salt, pepper and water; gradually add to tomato mixture. Stirring constantly, cook over medium heat for an additional 2 to 3 minutes. Add bread, stirring gently. Remove from heat; serve immediately. Serves 4 to 6.

Make your own fresh-tasting tomato juice fast!
Combine one part tomato paste to 3 parts cold tap
water...adjust water to suit your taste. Combine in blender
until smooth and creamy, add salt and pepper as desired.

Classic Comfort FOOD

Cream Corn Like No Other

Sherry Noble
Kennett, MO

For the richest flavor, you'll want to use whole milk for this recipe.

2 10-oz. pkgs. frozen corn,
   thawed
1 c. whipping cream
1 t. salt
1/4 t. pepper

2 T. sugar
2 T. butter, sliced
1 c. milk
2 T. all-purpose flour
1/4 c. grated Parmesan cheese

Combine corn, cream, salt, pepper, sugar and butter in a skillet over medium heat. In a mixing bowl, whisk together milk and flour; stir into corn mixture. Cook over medium heat, stirring constantly, until mixture is thickened and corn is cooked through, about 10 to 12 minutes. Remove from heat; stir in Parmesan cheese until cheese is melted. Serves 8.

If you don't have a small funnel handy for moving dry ingredients such as flour from bags to storage jars, use an envelope! For the "funnel" top, cut a large portion off of an envelope, then snip off its tip to insert into a jar.

Candie's Chicken & Dumplings

Jill Emery
Cedar Hill, TX

Mmm...I know what will be for dinner tonight!

14-1/2 oz. can chicken broth
5 to 6 c. water
3 to 4 boneless, skinless chicken
   breasts, cooked and diced
1 egg, hard-boiled, peeled and
   diced

1 t. ground cumin
salt and pepper to taste
2 12-oz. cans refrigerated
   biscuits

Combine broth and water in a large saucepan over medium-high heat; bring to a boil. Add chicken and egg. Stir in cumin, salt and pepper; bring to a boil. To make dumplings, pinch dough off by tablespoonfuls and roll into balls. Drop dumplings into broth mixture, one at a time, and cook for about 5 minutes. Serves 5 to 7.

Make quick dumplings by cutting flour tortillas in strips and then cooking them in chicken broth until tender.

Classic Comfort FOOD

Hunter's Pie

Heidi Maurer
Garrett, IN

*My 3-year old son Hunter loves this and my 8-year old son Luke
does too...without the beans!*

1 lb. roast beef, cooked
  and cubed
12-oz. jar beef gravy
8-oz. can sliced carrots, drained
8-oz. can green beans, drained

9-inch deep-dish pie crust,
  baked
11-oz. tube refrigerated
  bread sticks

Combine all ingredients except pie crust and bread sticks; spread
into pie crust. Arrange unbaked bread sticks on top, criss-cross-style.
Bake at 350 degrees for 20 minutes, or until bread sticks are golden.
Serves 4.

Save time on kitchen clean-up...always use a spatter screen
when frying in a skillet or Dutch oven.

Grandma's Casserole

Amy Creek
Tulsa, OK

Buy frozen chopped onions, from the freezer section, and precut bell peppers to make this even quicker to prepare.

1 lb. ground beef
1/4 c. onion, chopped
1/4 c. green pepper, chopped
6-oz. can tomato paste
10-oz. can tomatoes with chiles

15-oz. can creamed corn
8-oz. pkg. elbow macaroni,
  cooked
1 to 2 c. shredded Cheddar
  cheese

Brown ground beef, onion and green pepper in an oven-proof skillet over medium heat; drain. Add tomato paste, tomatoes with chiles and corn; mix well. Stir in cooked macaroni; mix thoroughly. Top with cheese and bake at 350 degrees until cheese is melted. Serves 4 to 6.

A trip to the salad bar makes quick work of any favorite recipe.
Buy just what you need of precut veggies and fruits, and even
mix up a fresh salad to go along with dinner.

Fast
Flavorful
Fiesta!

Quick-as-Lightning Enchiladas

Diane Stout
Zeeland, MI

I invented this recipe when I was short on time. When I serve this, everyone wants the recipe!

16-oz. jar chunky salsa
3/4 c. mayonnaise
4 c. cooked chicken, diced

8 to 10 8-inch flour tortillas
16-oz. pkg. shredded Colby-Jack
  cheese, divided

Mix together salsa and mayonnaise; stir in chicken. Spoon about 1/2 cup chicken mixture down the center of each tortilla; sprinkle each with 1/4 cup cheese and roll up. Place tortillas seam-side down in a greased 13"x9" baking pan. Spoon remaining chicken mixture evenly over top of tortillas. Sprinkle with remaining cheese. Bake at 350 degrees for 15 minutes, or until cheese is melted. Serves 4.

For extra-shiny glasses, add a little vinegar to the final rinse water either in the dishwasher or the sink.

Fast Flavorful Fiesta!

Santa Fe Pork Cutlets

Beverly Ray
Brandon, FL

What a delicious way to serve pork, and it's so fast!

3 T. all-purpose flour
1/4 t. salt
1/8 t. pepper
1 lb. pork tenderloin, sliced
    1/4-inch thick
3 t. oil, divided

1/2 c. salsa
1/2 c. frozen corn, thawed
1/4 c. water
1/4 c. sour cream
1/4 c. fresh cilantro, chopped

Combine flour, salt and pepper; dredge pork in flour mixture. Heat 2 teaspoons oil over medium heat in a non-stick skillet. Sauté half the cutlets for one to 1-1/2 minutes per side. Transfer to a plate. Repeat with remaining oil and cutlets. Cover to keep warm. Add salsa, corn and water to skillet. Simmer over medium heat for one minute. Remove from heat. Stir in sour cream and cilantro. Spoon salsa mixture over cutlets. Serves 4.

A spicy side in no time. Heat a 16-ounce bag of frozen corn in one teaspoon oil for 5 to 10 minutes. Stir in a 7-oz. jar of roasted red chiles, finely diced and one teaspoon each of cumin, chili powder, finely diced serrano chile and salt to taste. Heat through for 5 minutes...done!

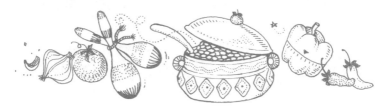

Chili-Tortilla Casserole

Sunny Hitshew
Fremont, CA

Speedy and good...some days are just meant for this quick dish!

16-oz. can chili with beans
2 10-3/4 oz. cans cream of
  mushroom soup
1 T. onion, minced

6 6-inch corn tortillas, torn into
  1-inch pieces
8-oz. pkg. shredded Mexican-
  blend cheese

Mix together all ingredients except cheese. Spread mixture in
an ungreased 13"x9" baking pan; top with shredded cheese. Bake at
350 degrees for 20 to 30 minutes. Serves 6.

Ranchito Tamale Casserole

Debbie Muer
Encino, CA

Substitute a can of sweet corn & diced peppers for added color.

5 large frozen beef tamales,
  thawed and crumbled
15-oz. can corn, drained
10-3/4 oz. can cream of
  mushroom soup
1 lb. ground beef, browned
  and drained

2 to 3 c. shredded Cheddar and
  Monterey Jack cheese
Optional: 4-oz. can diced green
  chiles

Arrange tamales in a lightly greased 2-1/2 quart casserole dish; top
with corn, soup, beef, cheese and chiles, if using. Bake at 350 degrees
until heated through, about 30 minutes. Serves 6 to 8.

Fast Flavorful Fiesta!

Fiesta Platter

Carolyn Lipham
Augusta, GA

My husband brought this recipe to our family and it is always a hit!
We enjoy it when we're on vacation and want great food that
doesn't take long to prepare.

1 lb. ground beef
1-1/4 oz. pkg. taco seasoning
14-1/2 oz. can tomatoes with
   chiles
10-1/2 oz. can chili without
   beans
16-oz. pkg. pasteurized process
   cheese spread, cubed

1 c. whipping cream
13-1/2 oz. pkg. tortilla chips
Garnish: shredded lettuce, diced
   tomatoes, sliced olives,
   chopped onion, sour cream,
   salsa

Brown ground beef in a large skillet over medium-high heat until no
longer pink; drain. Add taco seasoning, tomatoes and chili; stir well.
Reduce heat. Add cheese; stir until melted. Add whipping cream; mix
well. Simmer over low heat for 10 to 15 minutes, stirring occasionally.
Serve over tortilla chips; garnish with lettuce, tomatoes, olives, onion,
sour cream and salsa. Serves 6 to 8.

Never search for that twist tie again! Drop the twist tie in the
bottom of the kitchen trash basket before you put the liner in.
When you're ready to empty it, the tie is handy.

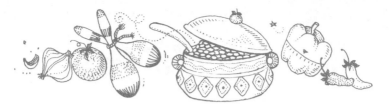

Sassy Salsa Rice

Theresa Lindquist
Gurnee, IL

We really enjoy this rice dish...what a nice change from the "usual!"

3 T. butter
2 c. long-cooking rice, uncooked

14-oz. can chicken broth
24-oz. jar salsa

Melt butter in a large saucepan over medium heat; add rice and sauté until golden. Add broth and salsa; bring to a boil. Reduce heat, cover and simmer for 15 to 20 minutes, until rice is tender and liquid is absorbed. Serves 6.

Tex-Mex Beans

Pam Massey
Marshall, AR

Even quicker when beef and onion are cooked ahead of time.

1 lb. ground beef or turkey
1 onion, diced
2 10-oz. cans tomatoes
    with chiles
2 15-oz. can pinto beans,
    drained and rinsed

13-1/2 oz. pkg. tortilla chips
Garnish: shredded Cheddar
    cheese, sour cream, salsa

Brown meat with onion in a skillet over medium heat for about 10 minutes, or until meat is no longer pink; drain. Add tomatoes; bring to a boil. Stir in beans and simmer over medium heat for 15 minutes, stirring often. Serve with tortilla chips and garnish with cheese, sour cream and salsa. Serves 8.

Fast Flavorful Fiesta!

Mexicana Veggie Bake

Tawnia Hultink
Ontario, Canada

Tasty layers topped with melted cheese.

1/2 c. green pepper
1/2 c. carrot peeled and finely
  chopped
1/2 c. celery, finely chopped
1/2 c. onion, finely chopped
2 c. cooked rice

16-oz. can refried beans
15-oz. can black beans
1 c. salsa
12-oz. pkg. shredded Cheddar
  cheese, divided

Sauté vegetables in a lightly greased skillet over medium heat for
5 minutes, or until tender. Remove vegetables to a large bowl; add
remaining ingredients except cheese. Layer half of mixture in a lightly
greased 13"x9" baking pan; sprinkle with half the cheese. Repeat
layering, ending with cheese. Bake at 350 degrees until heated
through, about 15 to 20 minutes. Serves 6.

Dress up a 16-ounce can of refried beans...it's easy! Just cook
2 seeded and diced pickled jalapeños, 2 chopped cloves garlic
and 1/4 cup chopped onion in 1/4 cup bacon drippings.
Add beans, heat through and stir in 1/2 teaspoon cumin.

Time for a Fiesta Soup

Marji Nordick
Meridian, ID

Ladle this soup into bread bowls...so good!

10-3/4 oz. can nacho cheese
   soup
10-3/4 oz. cream of chicken
   soup
2-2/3 c. milk
1 c. cooked chicken, diced
10-oz. can enchilada sauce

4-oz. can diced green chiles
15-oz. can black beans, drained
   and rinsed
1 c. frozen corn, thawed
Garnish: sour cream, tortilla
   strips and 1 bunch fresh
   cilantro, finely chopped

Combine all ingredients except garnish in a large saucepan; mix well. Cook over medium heat until heated through, about 10 minutes. Garnish as desired. Serves 6.

Tortilla Strips:

2 6-inch flour tortillas, cut into
   1/4-inch strips

1/2 t. oil

Spread strips on an ungreased baking sheet; toss with oil. Bake at 400 degrees for 10 to 12 minutes until crisp, stirring occasionally.

Keep your wooden cutting board in tip-top shape. Protect it from spills by coating with a thin film of olive oil and letting it soak in for a few minutes. Rub dry with a paper towel; repeat several times. Set aside the board for 24 hours before using again.

Fast Flavorful Fiesta!

Fast Flavorful Tortilla Soup

Pat Habiger
Spearville, KS

Simply pull 6 cans from the pantry shelf, some tortilla chips and cheese...that's it!

2 14-oz. cans chicken broth
10-oz. can chicken, drained
15-oz. can corn, drained
15-oz. can black beans, drained
   and rinsed

10-oz. can tomatoes with
   chiles, drained
13-1/2 oz. pkg. tortilla chips
Garnish: shredded Cheddar
   cheese

Combine all ingredients except chips and cheese in a large stockpot over medium heat; simmer until heated through, about 10 minutes. Serve over tortilla chips and garnish with cheese. Serves 6.

Chicken Chili

Mindy Humphrey
Evansville, IN

The flavor intensifies the longer it simmers. This recipe also freezes well!

2 T. oil
3 boneless, skinless chicken
   breasts, cubed
1 c. onion, chopped
1 c. green pepper, chopped
1/4 t. garlic powder
2 15-oz. cans stewed tomatoes
15-oz. can pinto beans, drained
   and rinsed

3/4 c. picante sauce
1 t. chili powder
1 t. ground cumin
1/2 t. salt
Garnish: shredded Cheddar
   cheese, sour cream, chopped
   avocado

Heat oil in a large pot over medium-high heat; add next 5 ingredients. Cook until chicken is no longer pink and vegetables are tender. Add remaining ingredients except garnish; bring to a boil. Reduce heat and simmer for 20 minutes. Top with cheese, sour cream and avocado. Serves 6 to 8.

Black Bean-Mango Salsa

Karen Smith
Charlotte, NC

This is also great as a side with grilled meat or any Mexican dish.

15-oz. can black beans, drained
    and rinsed
2 mangoes, peeled, pitted and
    diced
juice of 2 limes

1 jalapeño pepper, seeded and
    finely chopped
1/2 c. red onion, chopped
fresh cilantro to taste, chopped

Combine all ingredients in a medium bowl; let stand for 15 to
20 minutes for flavors to blend. Serves 4 to 6.

Weeknight Family Feast

Laura Craig
Woodlands, TX

One of our favorite "movie night" dinners.

14-1/2 oz. pkg nacho-flavored
    tortilla chips
2 15-oz. cans chili

1 c. shredded Cheddar cheese
Garnish: sour cream, salsa,
    sliced green onions

Cover bottom of soup bowls with tortilla chips; add one cup chili and
sprinkle with cheese. Microwave on high setting for 2 to 3 minutes,
or until cheese melts. Garnish as desired. Serves 4.

Fast Flavorful Fiesta!

Garden-Fresh Salsa

Staci Meyers
Cocoa, FL

I have added corn and black beans too...you can't go wrong.

14-1/2 oz. can diced tomatoes, drained
2 plum tomatoes, diced
3/4 c. green pepper, diced
1 jalapeño pepper, diced
1 T. fresh cilantro, finely chopped
1/3 c. sliced black olives
2 T. garlic, minced
1-1/2 T. lemon juice
1 T. lime juice
2 green onions, sliced
1/3 c. Spanish onion, diced
1/3 c. purple onion, diced
2 T. fresh parsley, finely chopped
salt and pepper to taste

Combine all ingredients; refrigerate until ready to serve.
Makes 3-1/2 to 4 cups.

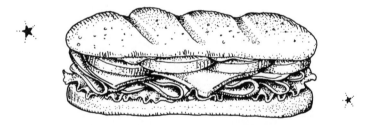

In Mexico, a quick meal is sometimes an overstuffed hero-style sandwich called a torta. Make your own by toasting split, hollowed-out crusty rolls under the broiler for about 3 minutes, turning once. Fill rolls with refried beans, avocado, pickled chiles, tomato, shredded cabbage, cooked meat, eggs or cheese. Serve them with salsa for authentic Mexican fast food!

Beef & Cheese Roll-Ups

Kaye Diener
Ashland, OH

Spinach is the "secret" ingredient...you'll love these!

1 lb. ground beef
1-1/4 oz. pkg. taco seasoning
   mix
10-oz. pkg. frozen spinach,
   thawed and drained
1 c. chunky salsa

3/4 c. shredded mild Cheddar
   cheese
8 10-inch flour tortillas,
   warmed
Optional: sour cream, shredded
   Cheddar cheese, taco sauce

Brown ground beef in a skillet over medium heat for 8 to 10 minutes,
or until no longer pink; drain. Add taco seasoning; mix well. Add
spinach and salsa; heat through. Remove from heat; add cheese. To
serve, spoon 1/2 cup beef mixture down center of tortilla. Roll up;
place seam-side down on serving dish. Repeat with remaining tortillas.
If desired, top with sour cream, cheese and taco sauce. Serves 4.

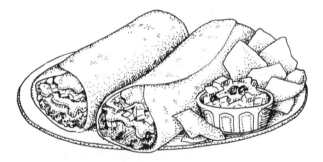

No one can resist fresh salsa and chips!
Pile blue and yellow tortilla chips in a colorful bowl,
placed in the middle of a large plate or platter. Don't forget
the tangy homemade salsa...what could be faster?

Fast Flavorful Fiesta!

Chicken Chimies

Diana Duff
Cypress, CA

Why go out to eat when this is just as good as any restaurant?

2 boneless, skinless chicken
  breasts, cooked and
  shredded
salt, pepper and garlic salt
  to taste
1 to 2 T. margarine
10 8-inch flour tortillas

8-oz. pkg. shredded Monterey
  Jack cheese
1/4 c. green onion, diced
1 T. oil
Garnish: sour cream, refried
  beans, guacamole

Sprinkle chicken with salt, pepper and garlic salt. Heat margarine in
a large skillet over medium heat; add chicken and sauté for about
3 minutes. Spoon chicken into each tortilla. Top with cheese and green
onion; roll up. Heat oil in a large skillet over medium-high heat. Add
rolled up tortillas and sauté until golden. Serve with sour cream, refried
beans and guacamole. Serves 6 to 8.

If you have a steam iron that no
longer steams, it might be
clogged with mineral deposits.
Try adding white vinegar in the
water reservoir, then set the iron
flat on an oven rack...place
sheets of newspaper underneath.
Plug the iron in and turn the
setting to "STEAM." By the
time the vinegar is steamed out,
your iron should be clean!

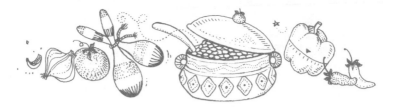

Chicken Ranch Jack

Sheila Wintermantel
Wellsville, OH

For a real kick, use hot pepper cheese!

2 to 3 T. butter
3 boneless, skinless chicken
   breasts, cut into strips
1/4 c. ranch salad dressing

6 slices bacon, crisply cooked
   and crumbled
1/3 c. shredded Monterey Jack
   cheese

Melt butter in a large skillet over medium heat; sauté chicken until cooked through. Remove from skillet. Arrange chicken in a lightly greased 2-quart casserole dish. Pour ranch dressing over chicken; stir well. Sprinkle with bacon and cheese; broil until cheese is melted and golden. Serves 4 to 6.

To freshen up your coffee maker, mix equal parts of white vinegar and water and pour inside. Let the machine run through its cycle, then refill with clean water; repeat. Do this once a month... and no more problem with mineral build-up!

Fast Flavorful Fiesta!

Mexican Pasta Salad

Kristin DeBusk
Davis, CA

This recipe is excellent whether served warm or cold and is super for potlucks or reunions. Sometimes I even combine different types of pasta for variety.

12-oz. pkg. rigatoni pasta, uncooked
14-1/2 oz. can Mexican-style stewed tomatoes, drained and liquid reserved
12-oz. pkg. Mexican pasteurized process cheese spread, diced

16-oz. can kidney beans, drained and rinsed
1/2 c. green pepper, chopped
1/3 c. sliced black olives
1/3 c. green onion, sliced

Cook pasta according to package instructions; set aside. Mix 2 tablespoons of reserved tomato liquid with cheese; microwave on high setting for 2 to 3 minutes, stirring occasionally, until cheese melts. Gradually blend in 1/3 cup reserved tomato liquid; discard any remaining liquid. Add pasta and remaining ingredients; mix thoroughly. Serves 6 to 8.

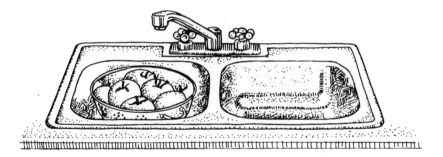

After cleaning your coffee maker with a water and white vinegar solution, pour the still-hot mixture over your kitchen faucets. The hot water will dissolve any remaining soap and the vinegar removes any lime deposits!

Walkin' Tacos

Karen Pilcher
Burleson, TX

Great for game day, picnics or anytime!

1 lb. ground beef
1-1/4 oz. pkg. taco seasoning
   mix
4 2-1/2 oz. pkgs. corn chips
2 c. lettuce, shredded

1 c. tomato, chopped
1 c. shredded Cheddar cheese
1/3 c. salsa
1/2 c. sour cream

Cook ground beef in a skillet over medium heat until browned; drain. Add taco seasoning and prepare according to package directions. Gently crush corn chips in unopened packages. Cut each bag open along one side edge. Spoon equal amounts of beef mixture and remaining ingredients into each bag. Serve in corn chip packages with a fork. Serves 4.

There's nothing like nachos for satisfying a hungry crowd.
Make 'em in no time by spreading 2 cups refried beans in a
jelly-roll pan. Arrange tortilla chips over beans, top with
1-1/2 cups cheese and jalapeño peppers to taste. Broil for
1 to 1-1/2 minutes, or until cheese is melted.
Top with salsa and sour cream...delicious!

Black Bean Mexican Pizza

Martha Little
Carrollton, TX

You'll be hooked on this!

10-oz. tube refrigerated
   pizza crust
15-oz. can black beans,
   drained and rinsed
3 T. olive oil
1 t. ground cumin
1/2 t. salt
1/8 t. ground ginger
1 t. hot pepper sauce

1/2 t. garlic, minced
2 T. fresh cilantro, chopped
2-1/4 oz. can sliced black olives,
   drained
1 c. shredded Monterey Jack
   cheese
1 c. shredded Colby cheese
1 c. chunky salsa

Roll pizza crust onto a greased 12" pizza pan; bake at 425 degrees for 7 to 10 minutes. In a food processor, combine beans, oil, cumin, salt, ginger, hot sauce, garlic and cilantro; process until smooth. Spread over crust; sprinkle with olives and cheeses. Bake at 425 degrees for 12 minutes; serve with salsa. Serves 6.

Set a microwave-safe cup half full of water inside the microwave, then turn on high setting for 2 minutes. The steam from the cup loosens any baked-on food for easy cleaning. Remember to let the cup cool for a minute before removing it from the microwave.

Chipotle Salad

Dawn Dhooghe
Concord, NC

Keep a bag of shredded carrots in the fridge to shorten prep time.

15-oz. can black beans,
   drained and rinsed
1 head Napa cabbage, shredded
1 carrot, peeled and thinly sliced
1/2 red onion, diced
1/4 c. fresh cilantro, chopped
2 chipotle peppers in adobo
   sauce, chopped

1/4 c. olive oil
2 T. balsamic vinegar
1 t. salt
1/2 t. pepper
10 10-inch flour tortillas

Combine beans, cabbage, carrot, onion and cilantro in a medium bowl. Toss to mix; set aside. In a small bowl, whisk together chipotle peppers, olive oil, vinegar, salt and pepper. Add to bean mixture; mix well. Cover bowl; refrigerate for 10 to 15 minutes. Warm tortillas; divide bean mixture among tortillas, roll up and serve. Makes 10.

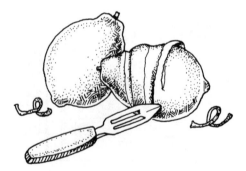

Homemade Citrus Vinegar is an amazing all-purpose cleaner!
Fill a glass quart jar with grapefruit, lemon, orange or lime
peels. Cover the peels with white vinegar and secure the jar lid.
Allow it to sit for 2 weeks occasionally shaking the jar.
Remove the peels and add 1/2 cup mixture to one gallon water.

Fast Flavorful Fiesta!

South-of-the-Border Salad

Mary Hall
Kentwood, MI

Go ahead...double or even triple the recipe!

1-1/2 lbs. ground beef
1-1/4 oz. pkg. taco seasoning
   mix
1/2 to 1 c. water
1 to 2 heads lettuce, chopped
15-oz. pkg. corn chips

2 tomatoes, chopped
1 onion, chopped
12-oz. pkg. shredded Cheddar
   cheese
favorite salad dressing
16-oz. jar salsa

Cook ground beef in a skillet over medium heat for 8 to 10 minutes, or until no longer pink; drain. Add taco seasoning and water. Simmer for 10 minutes; set aside. To assemble salad, layer as follows in individual bowls: lettuce, corn chips, beef mixture, tomatoes, onion and shredded cheese. Top with favorite dressing and salsa. Serves 4 to 6.

Spice up your favorite ranch salad dressing! To one cup of ranch salad dressing, whisk in 1/4 teaspoon chili powder and 1/2 teaspoon cumin. Let sit 5 minutes for flavors to blend.

Beefy Rice Bake

Annabelle Bone
Browns, AL

They'll ask for seconds!

1 lb. ground beef
1 c. instant rice, cooked
14-1/2 oz. can diced tomatoes
4-oz. can sliced mushrooms,
   drained

10-3/4 oz. cream of mushroom
   soup
1 T. Cajun seasoning
8-oz. pkg. shredded sharp
   Cheddar cheese

Brown ground beef in a large skillet over medium heat; drain. Add
rice, tomatoes, mushrooms, soup and seasoning; mix well. Cook for
5 minutes, or until heated through. Spread mixture in a lightly greased
13"x9" baking pan. Sprinkle with cheese and bake at 350 degrees for
10 minutes, or until cheese is melted. Serves 6.

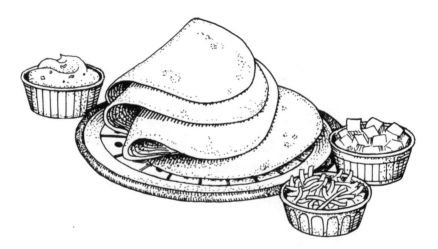

To crisp tortillas for filling, place a few teaspoons
of oil in a skillet and fry tortillas, one at a time,
for a few seconds until crisp. So simple!

Fast Flavorful Fiesta!

Nachos Magnifico

Jennifer Wood
Delaware, Ohio

Try something a little different...everyone will rave!

6 frozen beef tamales
16-oz. pkg. pasteurized process
   cheese spread, cubed
10-oz. can tomatoes with chiles
16-oz. pkg. nacho-flavored
   tortilla chips

1 c. tomato, diced
1 c. green onion, diced
1 c. sliced black olives
1/4 c. fresh cilantro, chopped

Heat tamales according to package instructions. Slice each tamale
into 4 slices; keep warm and set aside. Combine cheese and tomatoes
with chiles in a microwave-safe bowl. Heat on high setting for
9 minutes, or until cheese is melted. Mix well and keep warm. Spread
a single layer of tortilla chips on a lightly greased baking sheet. Spoon
one-third of cheese mixture over chips; top with one-third of tamale
slices and one-third each of tomato, onion and olives. Repeat 2 more
layers, ending with tortilla chips. Bake at 375 degrees for 2 minutes,
or just until heated through. Sprinkle with cilantro. Serves 4 to 6.

Mexican cheese is spicier than Cheddar or
American cheese. Check your local market or specialty store
and try some Queso Fresco, Queso Añejo or Chihuahua
for a real flavor of Mexico.

Fiesta Chicken Bake

Rene Summers
Pasadena, TX

I made some changes to an old family recipe and everyone loves it!

4 to 6 boneless, skinless
    chicken breasts, cooked
2 10-3/4 oz. cans cream of
    chicken soup
16-oz. container sour cream

10-oz. can tomatoes with chiles
1-1/2 c. shredded Monterey Jack
    cheese

Arrange chicken in an ungreased 13"x9" baking pan. Mix together
remaining ingredients; spread over chicken. Bake at 350 degrees for
25 to 30 minutes. Serves 4 to 6.

To bring out the best taste in meat, chicken or veggies
for Mexican recipes, grill them on an outdoor grill.
The flavor will really shine through!

Fast Flavorful Fiesta!

Easy Spanish Rice

Holly Sutton
Grahamsville, NY

Add cooked ground beef for a complete meal.

1 c. long-cooking rice, uncooked   16-oz. jar salsa
2 c. water   1 t. garlic, minced

Mix together all ingredients in a saucepan; bring to a boil over medium-high heat. Reduce heat to medium-low; cover and simmer for 20 minutes, or until tender. Serves 4 to 6.

Serve up authentic Mexican fruits & vegetables alongside dinner...jícamas, papayas, avocados and mangoes are all easy to find at the local grocery.

Easy Taco Pie

Marlene Darnell
Newport Beach, CA

The crescent roll dough gives this pie a deliciously flaky crust.

8-oz. tube refrigerated
  crescent rolls
1 lb. ground beef
1-1/4 oz. pkg. taco seasoning
  mix

16-oz. container sour cream
8-oz. pkg. shredded Mexican-
  blend cheese
14-1/2 oz. pkg. tortilla chips,
  crushed

Lay crescent dough flat on the bottom of an ungreased 8"x8" baking
pan. Bake according to package directions; set aside. Brown beef in
a large skillet over medium heat; add taco seasoning mix. Place beef
mixture on top of baked crescent dough. Layer with sour cream and
cheese; top with tortilla chips. Bake at 350 degrees for 10 minutes, or
until cheese has melted. Serves 8.

It's always best to wear rubber gloves when
cooking Mexican dishes that have hot peppers in the
ingredients. If you take a taste and it's too hot, try stirring
in a spoonful of sugar or a bit of salt and lime juice.

Fast Flavorful Fiesta!

Mexican Chicken & Broccoli

Patricia Tiede
Cheektowaga, NY

Try topping servings with some pineapple or peach salsa...yum!

12-oz. pkg. wide egg noodles,
  cooked
10-3/4 oz. can cream of
  mushroom soup
10-3/4 oz. can cream of chicken
  soup
2 c. cooked chicken, cubed

2 c. frozen chopped broccoli,
  thawed and drained
1-1/2 c. milk
2 T. dried, minced onion
16-oz. pkg. shredded Mexican-
  blend cheese

Combine all ingredients except shredded cheese in a lightly greased
13"x9" baking pan. Bake at 350 degrees for 20 to 25 minutes;
sprinkle with shredded cheese. Bake for an additional 5 minutes, or
until cheese is melted. Serves 4 to 6.

Cubed, cooked chicken can be purchased in vacuum sealed foil
pouches...just open and use in your favorite recipe.

Green Chile Con Queso Bake
Vickie

So quick & easy...you can get this dish to the table in record time!

1 10-pack frozen green chile
   and beef burritos
28-oz. can green enchilada
   sauce
8-oz. jar chile con queso

1 c. tomato, chopped
1 avocado, chopped
1 bunch green onions, chopped

Microwave burritos in a microwave-safe dish according to package directions; keep warm. Combine enchilada sauce and chile con queso in a small saucepan; bring to a simmer over medium heat. Spread 1-1/2 cups enchilada sauce mixture on a serving platter. Arrange burritos on top; spread remaining sauce over top. Sprinkle tomato, avocado and onions over burritos. Makes 10 servings.

An easy solution to remove coffee and tea stains from favorite china teacups. Try soaking them for 5 minutes in a solution of one gallon water to one teaspoon bleach.

Fast Flavorful Fiesta!

Sour Cream-Chicken Enchiladas

Sherri Fisher
Wichita, KS

Add some jalapeño slices...if you dare!

4 boneless, skinless chicken
   breasts, cooked and chopped
10-3/4 oz. can cream of
   mushroom soup
10-3/4 oz. can cream of
   chicken soup
8-oz. container sour cream

4-oz. can diced green chiles
1 onion, chopped
12-oz. pkg. shredded Cheddar
   cheese, divided
10 to 12 8-inch flour tortillas
1 c. water

Combine chicken, soups, sour cream, chiles, onion and 2 cups cheese
in a large bowl. Place a large spoonful of chicken mixture on each
tortilla; roll up. Arrange tortillas seam-side down in a lightly greased
13"x9" baking pan; set aside. Stir water into remaining chicken
mixture; pour over filled tortillas. Sprinkle with remaining cheese;
cover with aluminum foil. Bake at 350 degrees for 30 minutes.
Serves 4 to 6.

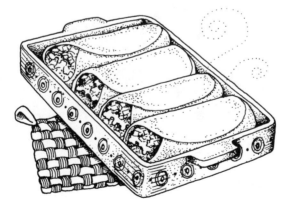

Freezer tip...never buy frozen food covered with frost.
It has probably been defrosted and refrozen.

Instant Hit Taco Dip

Deena Seegars
Pace, FL

My children want me to make this for every occasion...even if it's to celebrate our cat Lily's birthday. They love it that much!

16-oz. container sour cream
8-oz. pkg. cream cheese,
    softened
1-1/4 oz. pkg. taco seasoning
    mix
16-oz. jar salsa
1 head lettuce, chopped

8-oz. pkg. shredded Cheddar
    cheese
3.8-oz. can sliced black
    olives, drained
1 bunch green onions, chopped
13-1/2 oz. pkg. tortilla chips

Mix together sour cream, cream cheese and taco seasoning with an electric mixer at medium speed. Spread mixture in an ungreased 13"x9" baking pan. Layer salsa, lettuce, cheese, olives and green onions, in that order, over top of cream cheese mixture. Serve with tortilla chips. Makes 6 to 7 cups.

Remove pet hair in a flash! Simply slip on a damp rubber dishwashing glove and wipe your hand over sofas and chairs.

Super Supper Sandwiches

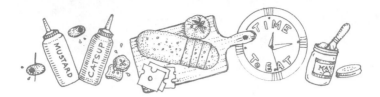

Tavern Burgers

Heather Daoust
Ashland, WI

Just as good as your favorite hamburger spot! No need to go out,
when you can have the tastiest burgers right at home.

1 T. oil
1 lb. ground beef
1 c. chicken broth
1 t. paprika
1 t. Worcestershire sauce

salt and pepper to taste
2 t. mustard
4 hamburger buns, split
1/2 c. onion, finely chopped
1 dill pickle, sliced

Heat oil in a skillet over medium heat. Add ground beef, breaking
apart as it cooks; drain. Add chicken broth, paprika, Worcestershire
sauce, salt and pepper; bring to a boil. Reduce heat to medium-low;
simmer for 15 minutes, stirring occasionally. Spread 1/2 teaspoon
mustard on top half of each bun; set aside. Spoon ground beef mixture
evenly among 4 buns; top with onion, dill pickle and top half of bun.
Serves 4.

Keep shopping simple...have a
shopping list that includes all
ingredients you normally use, plus
a few blank lines for special items.

Super Supper Sandwiches

Aloha Burgers

Jo Ann

Filled with flavor...you'll love these!

8-oz. can pineapple slices,
   drained and juice reserved
3/4 c. teriyaki sauce
1 lb. ground beef
1 T. butter, softened

4 hamburger buns, split
4 slices Swiss cheese
4 slices bacon, crisply cooked
4 leaves lettuce
1 red onion, sliced

Stir together reserved pineapple juice and teriyaki sauce in a small bowl. Place pineapple slices and 3 tablespoons juice mixture into a plastic zipping bag. Turn to coat; set aside. Shape ground beef into 4 patties and spoon remaining juice mixture over top; set aside. Spread butter on buns; set aside. Grill patties over medium-high heat to desired doneness, turning to cook on both sides. Place buns on grill, cut-side down, to toast lightly. Remove pineapple slices from plastic bag; place on grill and heat through until lightly golden, about one minute per side. Serve burgers on buns topped with pineapple, cheese, bacon, lettuce and onion. Serves 4.

Carry copies of favorite recipes with you so you can swing by the grocery and pick up the ingredients quickly and easily.

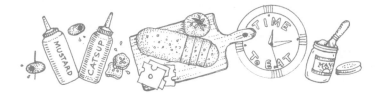

Quick Corned Beef Supreme

Sherry Svoboda
Abingdon, MD

This dish will be a hit with family & friends.
It's quick, easy and so yummy!

10 slices rye bread
1/4 to 1/2 c. Thousand Island
   salad dressing

1-1/4 c. creamy coleslaw
1 lb. sliced deli corned beef
1 lb. sliced Swiss cheese

Place 5 slices bread on a microwave-safe plate; spread each with one to 2 tablespoons dressing. Top each with 1/4 cup coleslaw, 3 to 4 slices corned beef and 2 slices Swiss cheese. Microwave on high setting for one minute. Continue to microwave for an additional minute, or until cheese melts and corned beef curls. Serves 5.

To save shopping time, call ahead and ask the butcher to cut and package special cuts of meat for you. Ready when you are!

Super Supper Sandwiches

Mom's Fried Bologna Sandwiches

Jackie Daunce
Lockport, NY

*When I was a kid and Mom would come home from work, my
3 brothers and I wanted dinner right away. Mom would take
off her coat, throw her purse on a chair and have this meal on the
table in 20 minutes or less!*

1 lb. bologna, thickly sliced
2 to 3 T. margarine
1 onion, sliced
2 14-1/2 oz. cans crushed
   tomatoes

salt and pepper to taste
hard rolls or rye bread

Cut each bologna slice into 8 wedges; set aside. Heat margarine in a
large skillet over medium heat; add onion and sauté until tender.
Remove from skillet; set aside. Add bologna and tomatoes to skillet;
cook over medium heat until heated through, about 5 minutes. Add
onion, salt and pepper. Serve on buttered hard rolls or rye bread.
Serves 4.

Sandwiches are wonderful.
You don't need a spoon or a plate!
-Paul Lynde

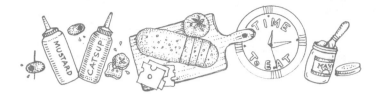

Crunchy Corn Salad

Sherry Rogers
Stillwater, OK

The perfect side for any sandwich!

2 15-oz. cans corn, drained
8-oz. can water chestnuts,
    drained and diced
2-oz. jar diced pimentos, drained
1 onion, diced
1/2 green pepper, diced
1/2 c. celery, diced

1 c. mayonnaise-type
    salad dressing
2 T. mustard
2 T. sweet pickle relish
1 c. shredded Cheddar cheese
Garnish: corn chips, crushed

Combine all ingredients except corn chips in a large bowl. Cover and chill until ready to serve. At serving time, top with crushed corn chips. Serves 4 to 6.

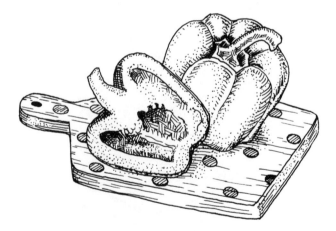

Stem and seed a green pepper in a flash...hold the
pepper upright on a cutting board. Use a sharp knife to
slice each of the sides from the pepper. You'll then have
4 large seedless pieces that can easily be chopped!

Greens Beans Caesar

Cheryl Lagler
Zionsville, PA

These savory green beans are ideal paired up with either hot or cold sandwiches.

16-oz. pkg. frozen green beans,
   cooked and drained
2 T. oil
1 T. red wine vinegar
1/4 t. salt
pepper to taste

1 clove garlic, minced
1 T. onion, chopped
1/4 c. butter, melted
1/4 c. soft bread crumbs
1/4 c. grated Parmesan cheese

Place green beans in an ungreased 2-quart casserole dish; set aside. Mix together oil, vinegar, salt, pepper, garlic and onion; pour over green beans. Toss to coat. In a small bowl, toss together melted butter, bread crumbs and cheese; sprinkle over top of beans. Bake, uncovered, at 350 degrees for 15 to 20 minutes. Serves 6.

Laundry that smells clothesline fresh and is
so soft...add 1/4 to 1/2 cup baking soda per load.

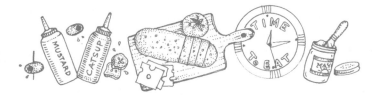

Mediterranean Chicken Wraps

Lynda McCormick
Burkburnett, TX

Just grill a few extra chicken breasts the next time you're making dinner and serve this wrap recipe the next day!

4 roma tomatoes, peeled and
   sliced
1/2 c. crumbled feta cheese
2 T. lemon juice
1/4 c. olive oil
sea salt and pepper to taste

4 boneless, skinless chicken
   breasts, grilled and sliced
4 whole-wheat flat breads
Garnish: lettuce, Kalamata
   olives, sliced red onion

Combine tomatoes, cheese, lemon juice and oil. Sprinkle with salt and pepper. Fold in chicken; arrange in flat bread. Top with Yogurt Sauce; garnish with lettuce, olives and onion. Serves 4.

Yogurt Sauce:

1 clove garlic, minced
3 T. chopped walnuts
1 t. olive oil

2 8-oz. containers plain yogurt
sea salt and pepper to taste

Mash garlic, walnuts and oil together with a fork. Mix into yogurt; sprinkle with salt and pepper.

Keeping bottled minced garlic on hand saves time when you're in a hurry. When swapping it for fresh, remember that 1/2 teaspoon equals one clove.

Super Supper Sandwiches

Garden Tuna Sandwiches

Jackie Smulski
Lyons, IL

*These yummy sandwiches put a little twist
on the traditional tuna salad.*

6-oz. can tuna, drained
1/2 c. cucumber, chopped
1/2 c. carrot, peeled and
   shredded
1/4 c. green onion, diced
1/4 c. mayonnaise
2 T. Dijon mustard

2 T. sour cream
1 T. lemon juice
pepper to taste
8 slices white or wheat bread
4 leaves lettuce

Combine first 9 ingredients in a bowl. Spread onto 4 slices bread; top
with lettuce leaves and remaining bread. Makes 4 sandwiches.

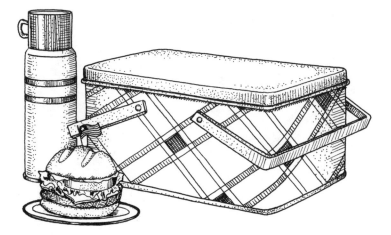

Tuna also comes in vacuum sealed foil pouches with no need
to drain. Ideal for camping or picnic fare.

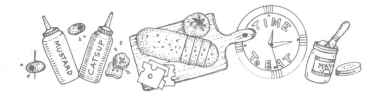

Grilled Salami Pizza Sandwiches

Sharon Crider
Junction City, KS

A family favorite for years!

2/3 c. pizza sauce
8 slices bread
4 slices deli salami

4 slices American cheese
garlic salt to taste
butter, softened

Spread pizza sauce on one side of 4 bread slices. Top each bread slice with one salami slice and one cheese slice; sprinkle with garlic salt. Top with remaining bread slices. Generously butter top and bottom of sandwiches. Heat a skillet over medium heat; add sandwiches and cook on both sides until bread is toasted and cheese is melted. Makes 4 sandwiches.

If a recipe calls for stewed tomatoes, take advantage of Mexican or Italian-style. They already have the seasonings added, so there are fewer ingredients for you to buy and measure!

Super Supper Sandwiches

Italian Subs

Robin Buzzard
East Earl, PA

This is a fun, easy alternative to the usual cook-out hot dogs and hamburgers...my family loves them!

1 lb. deli hard salami, diced
1 lb. deli salami, diced
1 lb. deli ham, diced
1 lb. pepperoni, diced
1 lb. provolone cheese, diced
1 head lettuce, chopped

dried oregano to taste
3/4 c. olive oil
1/4 c. vinegar
Garnish: sliced tomatoes, onion
6 sub buns, split

Combine meats, cheese and lettuce in a large bowl; sprinkle with oregano. Mix together oil and vinegar; toss with meat mixture. Spoon into sub buns and top with tomatoes and onion. Serves 6.

Here's a trick to remove white rings on furniture left by wet glasses. Make a thin paste of vegetable oil and salt.
Use your fingers to gently rub this mixture into the ring.
Let sit for an hour, then wipe off with a clean cloth.

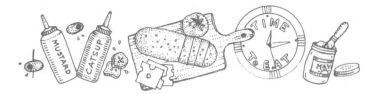

Crispy Apple Slaw

Elaine Nichols
Mesa, AZ

Very refreshing...a super sandwich side dish!

3/4 c. fat-free sour cream
1/4 c. sugar blend for baking
3 T. cider vinegar
2 T. ranch salad dressing mix
2 t. poppy seed
8-oz. pkg. shredded coleslaw
    mix

3 Red Delicious apples, cored,
    peeled and diced
3 green onions, thinly sliced
3 stalks celery, chopped
salt and pepper to taste

Whisk together sour cream, sugar blend, vinegar, dressing mix and poppy seed in a large bowl; set aside. Add coleslaw, apples, onions and celery; toss to coat. Cover and chill for at least 20 minutes. Add salt and pepper to taste. Makes 4 servings.

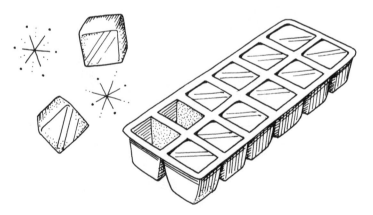

To keep Grandma's wicker furniture looking its best, add a small amount of oil soap to a bucket of warm water. Dip a soft-bristled brush into the bucket and carefully brush the furniture. Dry off the furniture with a soft cotton cloth.

Super Supper Sandwiches

Wilted Cabbage Salad with Bacon

Pat Habiger
Spearville, KS

A great recipe that's not only quick & easy, it's great-tasting too!

1/2 lb. bacon
1 onion, chopped
1 clove garlic, minced

1/2 c. tarragon vinegar
1 head cabbage, shredded

Cook bacon in a large skillet over medium-high heat until crisp; remove from skillet and crumble. Add onion and garlic to bacon drippings in skillet; cook until golden. Stir in vinegar and bring to a simmer. Add cabbage and bacon; sauté until heated through, about 2 minutes. Serve warm. Makes 8 servings.

To really speed up any recipe with crisply cooked bacon, purchase pre-cooked bacon. Just snip and add to salads or leave whole for sandwiches and burgers.

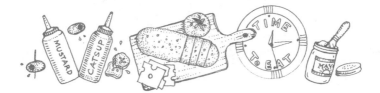

Chicken Ranch Quesadillas

Gretchen Brown
Forest Grove, OR

So simple to prepare! Pair it with a side of Spanish rice topped with diced tomatoes or refried beans sprinkled with shredded cheese.

1/2 c. ranch dip
8 8-inch flour tortillas
1 c. shredded Cheddar cheese
1 c. shredded Monterey Jack
   cheese

10-oz. can chicken, drained
1/3 c. bacon bits
Optional: salsa

Spread 2 tablespoons dip on 4 tortillas. Sprinkle each with one-quarter of Cheddar cheese, Monterey Jack cheese, chicken and bacon bits. Top each with remaining tortillas. Heat each tortilla in a lightly greased non-stick skillet until lightly golden; turn and heat until cheese is melted. Let stand for 2 minutes; slice into wedges. Serve with salsa, if desired. Serves 4.

It's said that ants will never cross a chalk line,
so get out the kids' chalk and draw a line by the door
or wherever ants tend to march!

Super Supper Sandwiches

Asian Chicken Wraps

Lisa Stanish
Houston, TX

These wraps are very easy to prepare after a long day at work,
not to mention they're so much tastier than fast food!

2 boneless, skinless chicken
  breasts, cooked and
  shredded
2/3 c. General Tso's sauce
1/4 c. teriyaki sauce
4 10-inch flour tortillas

10-oz. pkg. romaine and
  cabbage salad mix
1/2 c. carrot, peeled and
  shredded
4 T. sliced almonds
2 T. chow mein noodles

Combine chicken and sauces in a skillet. Warm over medium heat; set
aside. Divide ingredients evenly on each tortilla, beginning with salad
mix, carrots, chicken mixture, almonds and ending with chow mein
noodles. Roll up burrito style. Makes 4 wraps.

The next time you need an ice pack quickly, use a bag of
frozen vegetables out of the freezer!

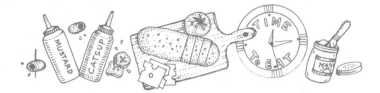

Philly Turkey Panini

Michelle Campen
Peoria, IL

Mmm...who says you can't have deli-delicious right at home?

8 slices rye or pumpernickel
   bread
2 T. butter, softened

1/2 lb. deli turkey, thinly sliced
4 slices mozzarella cheese

Spread one side of each bread slice with butter. Arrange 4 bread slices, butter-side down, in a skillet; top with turkey and cheese. Top with remaining bread slices, butter-side up. Cover and cook over medium heat for 4 to 5 minutes, turning once, until bread is crisp and cheese is melted. Serves 4.

Did you know that if you keep your candles in the freezer they will last longer and drip less?

Super Supper Sandwiches

Rosemary-Dijon Chicken Sandwiches
Vickie

Traditional chicken salad gets a brand-new twist!

3 c. cooked chicken breast,
   chopped
1/3 c. green onion, chopped
1/4 c. smoked almonds, chopped
1/4 c. plain yogurt
1/4 c. mayonnaise

1 t. fresh rosemary, chopped
1 t. Dijon mustard
1/8 t. salt
1/8 t. pepper
10 slices whole-grain bread

Combine all ingredients except bread, stirring well. Spread about
2/3 cup chicken mixture on each of 5 bread slices; top with remaining
bread slices. Serves 5.

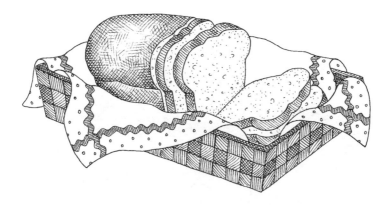

Some sandwiches can even be made ahead and frozen to help
trim time during busy weeks. Top bread slices with ham,
beef, chicken, turkey, cheese or even peanut butter.
Remember to leave off fresh toppers such as lettuce,
tomato and cucumber which don't freeze well.

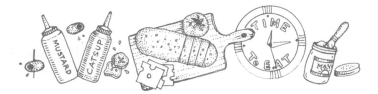

Super-Simple Pasta Salad

Linda Behling
Cecil, PA

*This pasta salad is a tasty take-along for a quick
sandwich & salad lunch.*

16-oz. pkg. penne pasta,
  uncooked
16-oz. pkg. cherry tomatoes,
  halved
1/2 c. black olives
8-oz. pkg. mozzarella cheese,
  cubed

4 to 5 leaves fresh basil,
  chopped
3 T. olive oil
salt to taste

Cook pasta according to package directions. Rinse cooked pasta with
cold water; drain and set aside. Combine tomatoes, olives, cheese and
basil in a large bowl. Add pasta; toss with olive oil and salt.
Makes 4 to 6 servings.

When toting a salad to a get-together,
keep it chilled by placing the salad bowl into
another larger bowl that is filled with crushed ice.

Sweet-and-Sour Green Beans

Anne Skalsky
Hartley, TX

*You'll bring out the best in any sandwich when you serve it
with these country-style beans.*

6 slices bacon
1 onion, chopped
2 14-1/2 oz. cans green
    beans, drained

3 T. oil
3 T. vinegar
3 T. sugar

Cook bacon in a large skillet over medium heat until crisp; remove
from skillet and crumble. Add onion to bacon drippings in skillet;
cook until tender. Mix together remaining ingredients; add to skillet.
Heat thoroughly; serve immediately. Makes 4 servings.

Coleslaw mix is easy to find in the
produce section and eliminates the time
you'd normally take to rinse and chop cabbage.

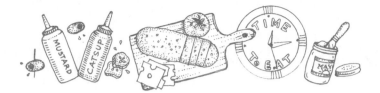

Cajun Chicken Sandwiches

Jeri Grant
Louisville, KY

Turn up the heat with Cajun seasoning and Pepper Jack cheese!

1/4 c. butter, melted
2 T. Cajun seasoning
4 boneless, skinless chicken
   breasts
4 slices Pepper Jack cheese

4 sandwich buns, split
8 slices bacon, crisply cooked
Optional: lettuce, mayonnaise,
   sliced tomato

Melt butter in a large skillet over medium heat; stir in Cajun seasoning. Add chicken; cook until juices run clear when pierced with a fork. Top with cheese; allow to melt. Serve on buns topped with bacon and, if desired, lettuce, mayonnaise and tomato slices. Serves 4.

If you're making a sandwich several hours before serving, first spread a light layer of softened butter, margarine or cream cheese on the bread. This prevents the bread from absorbing the moisture from the filling and becoming soggy.

Super Supper Sandwiches

Italian Sausage Sandwiches

Karen Venable
Lakeland, FL

Just like the scrumptious sandwiches you get at the county fair.

4 t. butter, softened
4 hoagie rolls, split
garlic powder to taste
1 lb. Italian sausage links
1 green pepper, sliced

1 onion, sliced
8-oz. pkg. shredded mozzarella
  cheese

Spread one teaspoon butter on each roll and sprinkle with garlic powder; place on an ungreased baking sheet butter-side up. Bake at 350 degrees until lightly toasted; set aside. Brown sausages in a large skillet over medium heat until cooked through; remove from heat. Add green pepper and onion to skillet; cook until tender, 2 to 3 minutes. Arrange sausages in rolls; evenly top with green pepper, onion and cheese. Place on baking sheet; bake at 350 degrees until cheese is melted. Serves 4.

To keep your white linens looking clean, chlorine bleach is a commonly used, but it can weaken fabrics. Bluing, which was once a staple in Grandma's laundry room, is often a better choice. Try adding it to your rinse water, it will give whites a very subtle blue hue making linens look brighter and whiter.

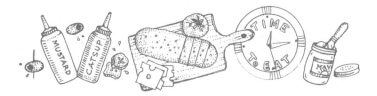

Ham Biscuits

Kristin Freeman
Jenks, OK

*Although made with dinner rolls, these sandwiches are
known as biscuits in the South. My aunt in North Carolina
shared this tasty recipe with me.*

24 brown and serve dinner rolls,
   split
16 slices Swiss cheese
12 slices deli ham
1/2 c. butter, melted

1 T. mustard
1 T. onion powder
1 T. Worcestershire sauce
1 T. poppy seed

On the bottom half of each dinner roll, layer 2 slices cheese,
3 slices ham and 2 additional slices cheese. Add top halves of rolls
and arrange on an ungreased baking sheet. Combine butter and
remaining ingredients; brush on tops of rolls. Bake at 350 degrees
for 15 to 20 minutes, or until cheese is melted and tops are golden.
Makes 24 sandwiches.

Combine one cup crushed dried lavender,
one teaspoon ground cloves, one teaspoon
ground cinnamon and 2 teaspoons baking
soda for a sweetly scented carpet freshener.
Shake mixture well to blend and sprinkle
on your carpet. Let it sit for one hour,
then vacuum up.

Super Supper Sandwiches

Chili Dog Wraps

Jen Eveland-Kupp
Blandon, PA

These are great for the kids!

10 6 or 8-inch flour or
    corn tortillas
10 hot dogs
16-oz. can chili

16-oz. jar salsa
1 c. shredded Cheddar or
    Monterey Jack cheese

Warm tortillas as directed on package. Place one hot dog and
3 tablespoons chili on each tortilla. Roll up tortillas; place seam-side
down in a greased 13"x9" baking pan. Spoon salsa over tortillas.
Cover and bake at 350 degrees for 20 minutes. Sprinkle with cheese
and bake, uncovered, about 5 minutes longer, or until cheese has
melted. Makes 10 servings.

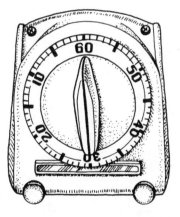

Get rid of marinara or chili sauce stains
in a plastic storage container by rubbing the stain
with a damp cloth dipped in baking soda. Or fill the stained
container with water, drop in one or 2 foaming denture
cleaning tablets, wait 20 minutes and rinse.

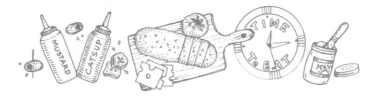

Avocado Potato Salad

Becky Drees
Pittsfield, MA

This salad is so good, it will be a "must-have" piled high on any sandwich platter!

6 redskin potatoes, cubed
2 avocados, pitted, peeled and
    chopped

2 T. lime juice
1/2 c. sweet onion, chopped
1/4 c. fresh cilantro, chopped

Cover potatoes with water in a large pan; bring to a boil over medium-high heat. Cook until tender. Drain and cover with cold water; drain well and place in a large salad bowl. Pour dressing over potatoes; toss and set aside. Toss avocados with lime juice; gently fold avocados, onion and cilantro into potatoes. Serve at room temperature. Serves 8.

Dressing:

1/2 c. plain yogurt
1/4 c. lime juice
2 T. honey mustard
1 T. olive oil

2 t. sugar
1 t. salt
1 t. pepper
2 cloves garlic, pressed

Whisk together all ingredients in a medium bowl.

Speed up the ripening of an avocado by placing it in a jar and completely covering with flour. Check it in a couple of days and if the skin gives a little and the avocado seems soft, it's just right.

One-Dish Delights

Bruschetta Chicken Bake

Renae Shingleton
Poca, WV

Skinless chicken strips mean short meal prep for this recipe!

14-1/2 oz. can diced tomatoes
   with basil and onion
6-oz. pkg. herb-flavored
   stuffing mix

1/2 c. water
1-1/2 lbs. boneless, skinless
   chicken breasts, cubed
1 c. shredded mozzarella cheese

Combine tomatoes, stuffing mix and water in a medium bowl. Stir just until moistened; set aside. Arrange chicken in a lightly greased 13"x9 baking pan; sprinkle with cheese. Top with stuffing mixture. Bake at 400 degrees for 20 to 25 minutes, or until chicken is cooked through. Serves 6.

Pick up prepared stuffing in the meat section at your grocer. It's ready to bake...you just top chicken breasts, stuff into pork chops or spoon alongside a turkey breast!

One-Dish DELiGhtS

One-Pot Chicken & Noodles

Joan Miller
Pottstown, PA

Comfort food...fast!

2 T. butter
3/4 lb. boneless, skinless
   chicken breasts, cubed
1/4 c. onion, finely chopped
14-1/2 oz. can chicken broth
6-oz. pkg. medium egg noodles,
   uncooked
10-oz. pkg. frozen peas
   and carrots

10-3/4 oz. can cream of
   chicken soup
3/4 c. milk
4-oz. jar chopped pimentos,
   drained
1/8 t. pepper
3/4 c. grated Parmesan
   cheese, divided

Melt butter over medium heat in a large saucepan; add chicken and
onion. Cook for about 5 minutes, or until chicken is cooked through.
Add chicken broth; bring to a boil. Stir in noodles and vegetables.
Cover and simmer over medium heat for 8 minutes, or until most of
liquid is absorbed, stirring every 2 minutes; set aside. In a medium
bowl, combine soup, milk, pimentos, pepper and 1/2 cup cheese; stir
until smooth. Add to noodle mixture; simmer until heated through.
Serve with remaining Parmesan cheese. Makes 6 servings.

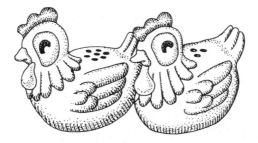

Freshen up the fridge! Clean the inside top to bottom using
warm, soapy water. You can even sprinkle some baking soda
into the water to make it even fresher.

Super Skillet Lasagna

Barbara Harris
Havelock, NC

I also like to use rotini, ziti and bowties in this recipe.

1 lb. ground beef
1 c. onion, chopped
1 clove garlic, chopped
salt and pepper to taste
2 T. Italian seasoning

15-oz. can tomato sauce
1 c. water
1 c. penne pasta, uncooked
1 c. shredded mozzarella cheese

Brown ground beef, onion and garlic in a large skillet over medium heat; drain. Sprinkle with salt and pepper; stir in Italian seasoning. Add tomato sauce and water; bring to a boil. Stir in pasta, cover and simmer for 10 minutes, or until pasta is tender. Sprinkle cheese over pasta; allow to melt. Serves 4.

A homemade salt scrub is the best way to clean cast iron.
Simply scrub the skillet or Dutch oven with coarse salt
and wipe with a soft sponge. Salt will give a thorough
cleaning, while preserving the pan's seasoning.
Simply rinse away salt and wipe dry.

No-Fuss Pierogi

Jackie Daunce
Lockport, NY

Mom has always been a good cook and this is one of her great Polish recipes simplified to get her in and out of the kitchen quickly.

1/2 onion, diced
1 T. margarine
16-oz. pkg. elbow macaroni,
    cooked

16-oz. container cottage cheese
salt and pepper to taste

In a large saucepan, sauté onion in margarine. Add macaroni, cottage cheese, salt and pepper. Cook over low heat for about 10 minutes, or until heated through, stirring often. Makes 4 servings.

Make it sparkle! To remove water spots off the shower door, wipe it down with a small amount of lemon oil each week.

One-Dish Speedy Couscous

Laurel Perry
Loganville, GA

Ready in a flash!

12-oz. pkg. couscous, uncooked
2 c. cooked chicken, diced
1 zucchini, chopped
1 stalk celery, thinly sliced
1 carrot, peeled and grated

2 c. orange juice
1/4 c. fresh basil, chopped
2 green onions, finely chopped
1/2 t. salt
1/2 t. pepper

Combine couscous, chicken and vegetables in a large serving bowl;
set aside. Bring orange juice to a boil in a saucepan over medium heat;
stir into couscous mixture. Cover tightly with plastic wrap; let stand for
5 minutes. Sprinkle with basil, onions, salt and pepper. Stir gently until
evenly mixed. Serves 4.

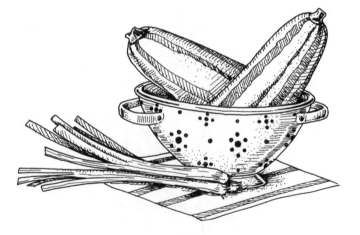

You probably have baking soda in your pantry...it will clean
and shine stainless steel sinks almost effortlessly.
Simply apply directly to surface and gently wipe.
Club soda works just as well!

One-Dish DELiGhtS

Garden-Fresh Zucchini & Tomatoes

Sherry Noble
Kennett, MO

Home-grown good!

2 slices bacon
8 zucchini, sliced 1/2-inch thick
1/2 red onion, thinly sliced
1/8 t. salt

2 tomatoes, cut into wedges
1/8 t. dried basil
pepper to taste
1/4 c. crumbled blue cheese

Cook bacon in a large skillet over medium heat until crisply cooked; crumble and return to pan. Add zucchini, onion and salt to skillet; stir frequently until zucchini is crisp-tender. Add tomatoes, basil and pepper; heat, stirring gently, until tomatoes are warm. Using a slotted spoon, transfer vegetable mixture to a serving bowl. Top with blue cheese. Serves 8.

If you accidentally peel too many potatoes for a recipe, cover the extras with cold water. Add a few drops of vinegar and keep refrigerated. They will stay fresh-tasting for 3 or 4 days.

Basil Caesar Salmon

Janice O'Brien
Warrenton, VA

When you want something a little extra special, but don't want to spend all day in the kitchen.

4 8-oz. salmon fillets
1/4 c. creamy Caesar salad
   dressing
pepper to taste
1 c. Caesar salad croutons,
   crushed

1/2 c. grated Parmesan cheese
2 t. dried basil
2 T. olive oil

Arrange salmon on a greased 15"x10" jelly-roll pan. Spread salad dressing over salmon; sprinkle with pepper. Combine croutons, Parmesan cheese and basil; sprinkle over and gently press on to salmon. Drizzle with oil. Bake, uncovered, at 350 degrees for 15 to 20 minutes, or until salmon flakes easily with a fork. Serves 4.

To clean baked-on food from a casserole dish, place a dryer sheet inside and fill with water. Let the dish sit overnight, then sponge clean. You'll find the fabric softeners will really soften the baked-on food!

One-Dish DELiGhtS

Grandma's Shrimp Creole

Linda Tilton
Gales Ferry, CT

A weeknight dinner treat.

1/4 c. butter
1 onion, chopped
1 green pepper, chopped
4 stalks celery, chopped
15-oz. can tomato sauce

1 T. vinegar
2 to 3 T. brown sugar, packed
1 lb. small shrimp, peeled and
    cleaned

Melt butter in a large skillet over medium heat; add onion, green pepper and celery. Sauté for 3 to 4 minutes; stir in tomato sauce and vinegar. Add brown sugar to taste. Simmer for 20 minutes. Add shrimp and simmer for an additional 5 minutes. Serves 6.

Bags of shredded lettuce make quick work of recipes.
Keep a bag on hand not only for crispy tossed salads,
but for layered dips, sandwiches and wraps.

Luau Delight

Pat Habiger
Spearville, KS

Serve this ham and sweet sauce over rice or noodles...kids love it!

2 T. butter
2-1/2 c. cooked ham, cubed
2 green onions, chopped
8-oz. can pineapple chunks,
    drained

1-1/3 c. pineapple juice
1 T. plus 1 t. cider vinegar
2 T. brown sugar, packed
2 t. mustard
2 T. cornstarch

Melt butter in a large skillet over medium heat. Add ham, onions and pineapple; sauté for 5 minutes and set aside. In a large bowl, combine pineapple juice, vinegar, brown sugar, mustard and cornstarch; mix well and pour over ham mixture. Cook over medium heat until heated through and thickened, about 5 minutes. Makes 4 servings.

A little dab of foam shaving cream can really help to remove red wine spills from carpets! Rub it in, then blot dry.

One-Dish DELIGhtS

Mom's Potato Casserole

Michele Zimmerman
Soap Lake, WA

*This recipe is one Mom created while her kids were growing up.
Now I make it for my kids and they love it as much as we did!*

4 cups potatoes, peeled, cooked
    and thinly sliced
1-1/2 t. salt
1/8 t. pepper
1/3 c. oil
3 T. vinegar

6 hot dogs, sliced 1/2-inch
    thick
1/4 c. onion, sliced
14-1/2 oz. can green beans,
    drained

Combine potatoes, salt, pepper, oil and vinegar. Layer sliced hot
dogs, potato mixture, onion and green beans in a greased 1-1/2 quart
casserole dish. Cover and bake at 400 degrees for 20 to 25 minutes.
Serves 4.

For quick clean-up, lightly spritz the outside of a grater with
non-stick vegetable spray.

Cheese & Spinach Tortellini Soup

Karen Perry
Englewood, CO

You can use your favorite beans in this recipe...just rinse them well.

2 T. olive oil
1/2 onion, diced
4 cloves garlic, minced
1 T. fresh thyme, chopped
1/4 t. red pepper flakes
6 c. chicken broth

8-oz. pkg. refrigerated cheese
   tortellini
9-oz. pkg. spinach
15-oz. can cannellini beans,
   drained and rinsed
1/2 c. grated Parmesan cheese

Heat oil in a large soup pot over medium-high heat; add onion, garlic, thyme and red pepper flakes. Cook until onion is soft, about 3 minutes. Add chicken broth; increase heat to high and bring to a boil. Stir in tortellini; reduce heat to medium and simmer for 4 minutes. Add spinach and beans. Simmer until spinach is wilted and tortellini is tender, about one minute. Ladle soup into bowls; sprinkle with cheese. Serves 6.

Rust stains in the tub or sink are easy to tackle.
Pour on hydrogen peroxide and sprinkle on a little cream
of tartar. Let it sit for a half hour, then wipe clean.

One-Dish DELiGhtS

Super-Simple Potato-Broccoli Soup

Barbara Pache
Marshall, WI

Whips up in minutes...oh-so good!

2 10-3/4 oz. cans cream of
    potato soup
10-oz. pkg. frozen broccoli,
    cooked

3 c. milk
16-oz. pkg. pasteurized process
    cheese spread, cubed
salt and pepper to taste

Combine all ingredients in a large saucepan over medium heat. Cook
without bringing to a boil, until heated through. Serves 6 to 8.

Easy Corn Chowder

Susan Owens
Redlands, CA

Top with a sprinkling of bacon bits if you'd like.

2 14-1/2-oz. cans new
    potatoes, drained and diced
2 15-oz. cans creamed corn
15-oz. can corn, drained

2-oz. jar diced pimentos, drained
16-oz. can chicken, drained
salt and pepper to taste

Combine all ingredients in a saucepan over medium heat. Cook until
bubbly, about 8 to 10 minutes. Serves 6.

Ahhh, soup & bread! Stop
by the bakery for a loaf of
bread. Warmed slightly in
the oven and topped with
real butter, it's heavenly
with any dinner!

Sausage Skillet Supper

Tracy Evans
Leesburg, OH

Dinner made with only 4 ingredients!

2 T. oil
16-oz. pkg. smoked sausage, sliced

6 potatoes, peeled and cubed
1 c. shredded Cheddar cheese

Heat oil in a large skillet over medium heat; add sausage and potatoes. Cook for 20 minutes, or until potatoes are tender. Sprinkle mixture with cheese; cover until cheese is melted. Serves 4.

Zucchini & Sausage Casserole

Donna Bebout
Edmond, OK

You can leave out the onion if you like...either way, this dish is super!

1 lb. ground pork sausage
1-1/2 c. instant rice, uncooked
2 c. zucchini, diced
1/2 c. onion, thinly sliced
16-oz. can stewed tomatoes

1 c. hot water
1 t. mustard
1 t. garlic salt
1/8 t. pepper
1 c. shredded Cheddar cheese

Brown sausage in a large skillet over medium heat. Drain, reserving 2 tablespoons drippings in skillet. Return sausage to skillet; add rice, zucchini and onion. Cook and stir until zucchini and onion are tender. Add remaining ingredients except cheese; bring to a boil. Cover; reduce heat and simmer for 5 minutes. Top with cheese; cover again until cheese is melted. Serves 4 to 6.

Fill the detergent cup in an empty dishwasher
with vinegar, then run on the rinse cycle.
A quick & easy way to keep it clean!

One-Dish DELiGhtS

Chicken Prosciutto Bundles

Elizabeth Cisneros
Chino Hills, CA

An elegant dinner...no one will believe just how quickly it's made!

4 boneless, skinless chicken
   breasts
8 leaves fresh basil
4 1/4-inch thick slices
   mozzarella cheese

1/4 t. salt
1/4 t. pepper
8 slices prosciutto or deli ham
1 T. oil

Cut a 3-inch pocket in thick side of each chicken breast. Place 2 basil leaves on each slice of cheese; sprinkle with salt and pepper. Stuff each chicken breast with a cheese slice. Wrap 2 slices prosciutto or ham around each chicken breast, securing with toothpicks. Heat oil over medium-high heat in a large oven-proof non-stick skillet. Add chicken and cook for 3 minutes per side, or until golden. Transfer skillet with chicken to oven and bake at 400 degrees for 12 to 15 minutes, or until juices run clear. Serves 4.

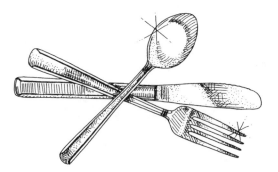

Remove tarnish on silver in no time. Sprinkle baking soda over silver, cover with boiling water and buff with a cotton cloth...sparkling!

Seaside Chowder

Kathleen Brillinger
South New Berlin, NY

I love to serve this chowder for tailgate get-togethers.

1/2 c. butter
1 lb. large shrimp, peeled and
   cleaned
3 6-1/2 oz. cans chopped clams
2 10-1/2 oz. cans she-crab soup
2 18.8-oz. cans chunky clam
   chowder

1/4 t. pepper
1/2 c. vermouth or white grape
   juice
fresh parsley to taste

Heat butter in a large soup pot over medium heat. Add shrimp; sauté until opaque. Stir in remaining ingredients; reduce heat and simmer until heated through, about 10 to 15 minutes. Serves 6 to 8.

Dilly Tomato Soup

Leah-Anne Schnapp
Effort, PA

Go ahead...make a grilled cheese sandwich to go along with this!

2 10-3/4 oz. cans tomato soup
3/4 c. low-fat plain yogurt
1/2 c. half-and-half

3/4 c. water
1 T. fresh dill, finely chopped

Combine all ingredients in a medium saucepan over medium heat. Simmer until heated through, about 10 minutes, without bringing to a boil. Serves 4.

Doing a little spring cleaning?
Fill a bucket with cleaning must-haves
and tote it from room to room.
Hang rubber gloves over the rim
to dry...so simple!

One-Dish DELiGhtS

Charlotte's Chicken-Asparagus Casserole

J.J. Presley
Portland, TX

A good friend, Charlotte, who is no longer with us was a wonderful cook and shared this recipe with me.

8-oz. pkg. pasteurized process
   cheese spread, diced
10-3/4 oz. can cream of
   mushroom soup
1 c. cooked chicken, cubed

2-oz. jar diced pimentos, drained
15-oz. can asparagus, drained
3/4 c. saltine crackers, crushed
2 t. butter, diced

Combine cheese and soup in a saucepan over low heat. Cook until cheese is melted, about 6 to 8 minutes. Stir in chicken and pimentos. Spread mixture in an ungreased 2-quart casserole dish; arrange asparagus over top. Sprinkle cracker crumbs over asparagus and dot with butter. Bake at 350 degrees until golden, about 20 to 25 minutes. Serves 4 to 6.

To make kitchen glasses crystal clear, soak them
in plain white distilled vinegar, then rinse.

Saucy Beef Skillet

Dottie Liwai
Durant, OK

Such tender beef...absolutely wonderful!

1/2 t. sugar
2 t. cornstarch
1-1/2 T. dry sherry or
    orange juice
3 T. oyster sauce

2 T. peanut oil
2 lbs. beef round steak, thinly
    sliced
6 green onions, sliced 1/2-inch
    thick pieces

Mix together sugar, cornstarch, sherry or orange juice and oyster sauce; set aside. Heat oil in a large skillet over medium heat; add steak and cook for about 3 minutes. Stir in sherry mixture. Add green onions and cook for an additional 10 minutes, or until steak is cooked through and onions are tender. Serves 4.

Here's how to keep fresh-picked flowers looking perky.
Scrub flower vases with a solution of water and
bleach...sure to keep the vase clean.

One-Dish DELiGhtS

Chinese Fried Rice

Irene Robinson
Cincinnati, OH

I think this is a wonderful (and tasty!) way to use leftovers I have on hand.

3 T. oil
1 c. cooked chicken, pork or
   shrimp, chopped
2 eggs, beaten
3/4 t. salt

1/2 t. pepper
3 c. cooked rice, chilled
2 T. soy sauce
2 green onions, snipped

Heat oil in a deep skillet over medium heat. Add meat and cook for one minute. Add eggs, salt and pepper; cook, stirring constantly, until eggs are set. Add rice and soy sauce; cook, stirring constantly, for about 5 minutes, until rice is heated through. Garnish with green onions. Makes 4 to 6 servings.

Your disposal can be cleaned up in a jiffy. Pour white vinegar into an ice cube tray (used just for this) and freeze. Drop the cubes, one at a time, into the disposal while it's running.

Crunchy Ranch Chicken

Marla Caldwell
Forest, IN

Simply mix, dip, cook...what a kid pleaser!

8-1/2 oz. pkg. cornbread
   muffin mix
1-oz. pkg. ranch salad
   dressing mix

1 c. milk
6 boneless, skinless chicken
   breasts
2 T. oil

Combine cornbread mix and salad dressing mix in a large plastic zipping bag; set aside. Pour milk into a shallow bowl. Dip chicken into milk; place in cornbread mixture and shake to coat. Heat oil in a large skillet over medium heat. Add chicken; cook until golden on both sides, about 6 to 7 minutes per side, or until juices run clear. Serves 6.

If your favorite non-stick skillet is sticky, boil
2 tablespoons baking soda with 1/2 cup vinegar
and one cup water in it for a few minutes.
Rinse well with hot water and wipe clean.

One-Dish DELiGhtS

Kielbasa & Peppers

Carolyn Black
Fresno, CA

I like to spoon this over rice and serve with a tossed salad.

2 T. olive oil
2 lbs. Kielbasa, sliced 1/2-inch
   thick
1 red pepper, sliced into strips

1 green pepper, sliced into strips
1 yellow pepper, sliced into
   strips
1 onion, halved and sliced

Heat oil in a large skillet over medium heat; add Kielbasa. Sauté for 3 minutes; add vegetables. Cook until Kielbasa is golden and vegetables are tender, about 8 to 10 minutes. Serves 4 to 6.

To keep your stainless steel sink in tip-top shape, don't leave rubber mats in the sink or use steel wool to remove stains. After cleaning the sink, it's always a good idea to rinse and wipe it dry.

Balsamic Chicken & Pears

Shirl Parsons
Cape Carteret, NC

The flavors in this dish blend together so well...very, very tasty.

2 t. oil, divided
4 boneless, skinless chicken
  breasts
2 Bosc pears, cored and cut into
  8 wedges

1 c. chicken broth
3 T. balsamic vinegar
2 t. cornstarch
1-1/2 t. sugar
1/4 c. dried cherries or raisins

Heat one teaspoon oil in a large non-stick skillet over medium-high heat; add chicken. Cook until golden and cooked through, about 4 to 5 minutes per side. Transfer to a plate; keep warm. Heat remaining oil in same skillet; add pears and cook until tender and golden. In a small bowl, combine remaining ingredients except cherries or raisins. Stir broth mixture into skillet with pears; add cherries or raisins. Bring to a boil over medium heat; cook for one minute, stirring constantly. Return chicken to pan; heat through. Serves 4.

After boiling chicken, freeze reserved broth in an
ice cube tray or plastic container. Just thaw, then toss
into any recipe calling for broth.

One-Dish DELiGhtS

Tangy Chicken Piccata

Barb Bargdill
Gooseberry Patch

Great served with rice and a spinach salad.

1 lb. boneless, skinless chicken
    breasts
2 T. all-purpose flour
1/2 c. orange juice
1/4 c. honey mustard
1/4 c. orange marmalade
1/4 t. dried rosemary, crushed
1 orange, peeled, thinly sliced
    and quartered

Dredge chicken in flour; set aside. Heat a lightly greased skillet over medium heat; add chicken and cook for 5 minutes, or until golden. Add juice, mustard, marmalade and rosemary; bring to a boil. Reduce heat; simmer for 5 minutes. Stir in orange slices and heat through. Serves 4.

Did you know that a dab of nail polish remover
will take paint spatters off windows?

White Cheddar-Cauliflower Casserole

Lisa Ashton
Aston, PA

*Lots of cheese and bacon will have the kids eating their veggies
in this terrific casserole.*

1 head cauliflower, cooked and
    mashed
8-oz. pkg. white Cheddar
    cheese, grated and divided
1/2 lb. bacon, crisply cooked and
    crumbled, divided

1/2 c. cream cheese, softened
2 T. sour cream
salt and pepper to taste

Combine cauliflower, half the Cheddar cheese and three-quarters
of bacon in a medium bowl. Add cream cheese and sour cream; mix
well. Spread mixture in a greased 8"x8" baking pan; top with
remaining cheese and bacon. Sprinkle with salt and pepper. Bake,
uncovered, at 350 degrees for 20 to 25 minutes, until golden around
edges. Serves 6.

When butter is too cold to spread, turn a hot bowl over the
butter dish. It will soften, but not melt.

One-Dish DELiGhtS

Green Beans with a Twist

Crystal Hamlett
Amory, MS

If you'd like, add some chopped onion to the green beans while they're cooking.

2 T. butter
16-oz. pkg. frozen French-cut
   green beans, thawed
1 c. sliced mushrooms

1-oz. pkg. ranch salad dressing
   mix
4 slices bacon, crisply cooked
   and crumbled

Heat butter in a large skillet over medium heat; add green beans and mushrooms. Sauté for 10 minutes, or until tender. Sprinkle with ranch dressing mix; toss to coat. Top with bacon. Serves 6.

Waikiki Rice

Sharon Crider
Junction City, KS

Ready in 10 minutes!

9-oz. can pineapple tidbits
1-1/3 c. water
1/4 c. brown sugar, packed
2 T. margarine, sliced

1/2 t. salt
1/8 t. cinnamon
1-1/3 c. instant rice, uncooked

Combine pineapple with juice and remaining ingredients except rice in a saucepan. Bring to a boil over medium-high heat; stir in rice. Reduce heat, cover and simmer for 10 minutes. Makes 6 servings.

If you store fresh pineapple at room temperature for one or 2 days before slicing, it will become softer and sweeter.

Roasted Salmon with Citrus & Herbs

Karen Ensign
Providence, UT

Really nice served with some grilled asparagus.

1 T. fresh parsley, chopped
1 T. fresh thyme, chopped
1 T. garlic, minced
1 T. olive oil
2 t. lemon zest

2 t. lime zest
1-1/2 t. salt
1/2 t. pepper
2 to 3-lb. salmon fillet

Combine all ingredients except salmon in a small bowl; set aside. Arrange salmon on a parchment paper-lined baking sheet; spread herb mixture over salmon. Bake at 400 degrees for 12 to 15 minutes, or until salmon flakes easily with a fork. Serves 4 to 6.

Non-stick pots & pans scratch easily, so always use wood or plastic utensils when cooking...don't use metal!

One-Dish DELiGhtS

Baked Fish Au Gratin

Marla Caldwell
Forest, IN

I like to use tilapia for this recipe, but the mild taste of red snapper, rockfish and whitefish is also ideal for this delicately flavored dish.

1 lb. fresh or frozen fish fillets, thawed
1/4 c. dry bread crumbs
1/4 t. lemon-pepper seasoning
1/2 c. shredded Cheddar cheese

Arrange fish in a lightly greased 13"x9" baking pan; set aside. In a small bowl, combine bread crumbs and seasoning. Spoon bread crumb mixture over fish. Bake, uncovered, at 400 degrees for 15 to 20 minutes, or until fish flakes easily with a fork. Sprinkle with cheese; bake for an additional 5 minutes, or until cheese melts. Serves 4.

You can quickly clean baking pans that fish was prepared in...just pour white vinegar into the hot baking pan and let sit several minutes before cleaning.

Oriental Steak

Katie Shrider-Eviston
San Diego, CA

Order some egg rolls to go along with this dinner.

1/4 c. oil
1-1/2 lbs. boneless beef sirloin,
   sliced 1/4-inch thick
1 green pepper, sliced
1 red or yellow pepper, sliced
1 onion, sliced
2 stalks celery, sliced

1 clove garlic, minced
14-1/2 oz. can diced tomatoes
1-1/2 c. catsup
1/2 c. Worcestershire sauce
1/4 to 1/2 c. water
cooked rice or egg noodles

Heat oil in a large pan over medium heat; add beef, peppers, onion, celery and garlic. Cook until beef is browned and vegetables are crisp-tender, about 8 minutes. Add tomatoes with juices, catsup and Worcestershire sauce; mix well. Cover and cook over low heat for 15 to 20 minutes, until thickened. Add water as needed to desired consistency. Serve over rice or noodles. Serves 4 to 6.

Freshen the fridge with a combination of one quart
warm water mixed with one tablespoon borax.
Perfect for sponging down shelves and crisper drawers.

One-Dish DELiGhtS

Chicken & Brown Rice Pilaf

Jessica Robertson
Fishers, IN

Fast & full of flavor!

1 T. oil
4 boneless, skinless chicken
   breasts
10-1/2 oz. can chicken broth
1/2 c. water

1 c. sliced mushrooms
1 onion, chopped
1 c. frozen peas
2 c. instant brown rice,
   uncooked

Heat oil in a large skillet over medium heat; add chicken. Cook until golden, about 4 to 6 minutes per side. Remove from skillet and set aside. Add broth and water to skillet; bring to a boil over medium heat. Stir in remaining ingredients; top with chicken and cover. Reduce heat to low and cook for 5 minutes, or until chicken is cooked through. Let stand 5 minutes. Serves 4.

Store mushrooms in the refrigerator unwashed and dry. Placed in a paper bag, not plastic, will keep them fresher longer.

Reuben Casserole

Beverly Deardorff
Tulsa, OK

Favorite sandwich ingredients turn into a savory casserole!

14-oz. can sauerkraut
2 tomatoes, thinly sliced
2 T. Thousand Island salad
   dressing
2 T. margarine
2 4-oz. pkgs. deli-sliced corned
   beef, shredded

2 c. shredded Swiss cheese
16.3-oz. tube refrigerated flaky
   biscuits
2 rye crackers, crushed
1/4 t. caraway seed

Spread sauerkraut with juice in an ungreased 13"x9" baking pan; top with tomato slices. Dot with dressing and margarine; arrange corned beef on top. Sprinkle with cheese. Bake at 425 degrees for 15 minutes; remove from oven. Separate each biscuit into 3 layers; arrange on top of cheese. Sprinkle with rye cracker crumbs and caraway seed. Bake for an additional 8 to 10 minutes, or until golden. Serves 4 to 6.

Try this tip to keep cheese moisture-free...add a
few sugar cubes in a plastic zipping bag with the cheese. When
the cubes get soggy in a few days, replace them. This keeps
cheese fresher longer.

One-Dish DELiGhtS

Texas-Style Ranch Stew

Nancy Brown
Cypress, TX

Hearty and filling...you'll be doing the 2-step when you taste this!

1-1/2 lbs. ground beef
1/2 onion, chopped
2 15-oz. cans ranch-style beans
hot pepper sauce to taste
16-oz. pkg. frozen corn

1/4 c. water
8-oz. pkg. shredded Colby-Jack
   cheese

Cook beef and onion together in a large skillet over medium heat until browned; drain. Stir in beans and hot pepper sauce; set aside. Place corn and water in a microwave-safe bowl; microwave on high setting for 4 minutes. Add to stew. Stir in cheese until melted; simmer for an additional 5 minutes over medium heat. Serves 6 to 8.

When you need raw onion slices for a recipe, slice the onion a day early and place the slices into a glass jar. Fill the jar with cold water, cover and refrigerate...this keeps onion slices crisp and takes away some of the strong taste!

Chicken Parmesan

Sara Zimdars
Fredonia, WI

Serve this with some crusty rolls and a fresh veggie...so good.

4 boneless, skinless chicken
   breasts
2 14-1/2 oz. cans diced
   tomatoes with basil, garlic
   and oregano

2 T. cornstarch
1/4 t. hot pepper sauce
1/3 c. grated Parmesan cheese

Arrange chicken in a 13"x9" baking pan that has been sprayed with non-stick vegetable spray. Cover with aluminum foil; bake at 425 degrees for 20 minutes. Remove aluminum foil; drain and set aside. Combine tomatoes, cornstarch and hot pepper sauce in a saucepan over medium heat. Cook, stirring constantly, until thickened and cornstarch is dissolved. Pour tomato mixture over chicken; top with cheese. Bake at 425 degrees, uncovered, for 5 minutes, or until chicken is done. Makes 4 servings.

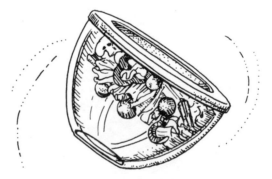

Serving salad alongside dinner tonight? Tear greens and place in a large plastic bowl with a tight-fitting lid. Add any favorite salad toppers and dressing, then tighten the lid and shake to toss.

Spaghetti Carbonara

Marc Magee
Madison, CT

*This recipe is one our teenage son likes to prepare for our family.
It's become a favorite dinner to enjoy after a football or hockey game.*

16-oz. pkg. thin spaghetti,
   uncooked
8 to 10 slices turkey bacon,
   finely chopped
3 cloves garlic, minced
2/3 c. dry white wine or
   chicken broth

1 c. pasteurized egg substitute
1/3 c. fresh parsley, chopped
1/3 c. grated Parmesan cheese
salt and pepper to taste

Prepare spaghetti according to package directions; drain and set aside.
Cook bacon and garlic in a small pan over medium-low heat for 3 to
4 minutes, until golden. Add wine or broth to pan; increase heat and
bring to a boil. Cook until mixture is reduced by half; pour into a large
serving bowl. Let cool for 5 minutes. Stir in egg substitute and parsley;
mix well. Add cooked spaghetti and cheese; toss to coat. Sprinkle with
salt and pepper. Serves 4.

You can keep pasta dishes light by preparing them
with flavorful vegetables and herbs rather than
meats and cream sauces.

Pizza & Pasta... PRONTO!

Penne Rustica

Dawn Kozlowski
Silver Creek, NY

A salad, a loaf of bread and a big plate of this penne is heavenly!

1/4 c. olive oil
1-1/2 T. garlic, minced
1/2 c. onion, diced
3 c. broccoli flowerets, cut into
    bite-size pieces

1 c. chicken broth
16-oz. pkg. penne pasta, cooked
1/3 c. grated Parmesan cheese
salt and pepper to taste

Heat oil in a large skillet over medium heat; add garlic, onion and broccoli. Cook for 7 minutes, or until broccoli is tender. Add broth; simmer for 2 minutes. Place pasta in a large bowl; add broccoli mixture, cheese, salt and pepper. Toss to coat. Serves 6.

Shine up brass knobs, hinges and fixtures in a jiffy. If they're lacquered, just clean with a damp cloth. If unlacquered, use a commercial metal cleaner...never strong abrasives.

Pepperoni-Pasta Bake

Tammy Steinert
Hoisington, KS

With only 2 of us, I often freeze any leftovers
for a quick meal when time is short.

1 lb. ground beef, browned
and drained
8-oz. pkg. mostaccioli pasta,
cooked
26-oz. jar spaghetti sauce

8-oz. pkg. shredded mozzarella
cheese, divided
1/4 c. pepperoni, diced
salt and pepper to taste

Combine ground beef, mostaccioli, spaghetti sauce, 1-1/2 cups
mozzarella and diced pepperoni in a large bowl. Sprinkle with salt and
pepper. Spread in a lightly greased 13"x9" baking pan; top with
remaining cheese. Bake at 350 degrees for 15 to 20 minutes, or until
cheese is melted. Serves 4 to 6.

Colanders can get sticky and hard to clean after draining
pastas. To prevent this, coat the colander with a non-stick
vegetable spray before using!

Pizza & Pasta... PRONTO!

American Spaghetti

Dale-Harriet Rogovich
Madison, WI

I remember my mother making this dish when I was a very little girl.

16-oz. pkg. spaghetti, uncooked
2 15-oz. cans chunky-style
    tomato sauce

1/2 lb. American cheese, cubed
Optional: grated Parmesan
    cheese

Prepare spaghetti according to package directions; drain without rinsing and return to pan. Stir in tomato sauce. Stir in cubed cheese; cook and stir on low until cheese melts. Sprinkle with Parmesan, if desired. Serves 3 to 4.

Don't worry about preparing too much pasta!
Any leftovers can be refrigerated and used later
in other dishes, like salads, casseroles or soups.

Basil-Mushroom Pizza

Laurel Perry
Loganville, GA

You may just have to make more than one for dinner...it's that good!

2 T. butter
1 c. portabella mushrooms, sliced
2 cloves garlic, minced
12-inch Italian pizza crust
3 T. olive oil

1 c. spinach, sliced into 1/2-inch strips
1/2 c. fresh basil, chopped
8-oz. pkg. shredded mozzarella cheese

Melt butter in a large skillet over medium heat. Add mushrooms and garlic; sauté just until tender, about 5 minutes. Place pizza crust on an ungreased baking sheet; brush with olive oil. Sprinkle spinach evenly over pizza crust, followed by basil, mozzarella and mushroom mixture. Bake at 350 degrees for 8 to 10 minutes, or until cheese is melted and edges of pizza are crisp. Makes 4 servings.

If you like garlic-flavored oil, try this. Peel fresh garlic cloves, place in a glass jar and cover with sesame or safflower oil. The delicious oil is terrific for cooking and for salads! Remember to keep the jar in the fridge and use within 10 days.

Pizza & Pasta... PRONTO!

Spinach Salad Pizzas

Cheryl Lagler
Zionsville, PA

*I enjoyed this at a restaurant and decided to create
my own version at home!*

2 10-1/8 oz. pkgs. frozen French bread cheese pizzas	8-oz. pkg. sliced mushrooms
8-oz. pkg. baby spinach	1 cucumber, diced
1 tomato, chopped	6 T. ranch salad dressing

Bake pizzas according to package directions; place pizzas on
4 serving plates. Top each pizza with one-quarter each of the spinach,
tomato, mushrooms and cucumber. Drizzle 1-1/2 tablespoons ranch
salad dressing over each pizza. Serves 4.

If you want to soak pots & pans overnight, but the water runs
out of the kitchen sink too quickly, place a piece of plastic wrap
under the drain stopper to make a tight seal.

Pepperoni Bread Sticks

Tracy McIntire
Delaware, OH

Serve with a variety of dipping sauces...marinara, ranch, blue cheese.

2 c. biscuit baking mix
1/2 c. water
1/2 c. pepperoni, chopped

1/4 c. butter, melted
1 T. grated Parmesan cheese
26-oz. jar spaghetti sauce

Mix together baking mix, water and pepperoni until dough forms. Turn dough onto surface dusted with baking mix; gently roll in baking mix to coat. Knead 5 times. Roll dough out into a 10-inch square; cut in half. Cut each half crosswise into 14 strips. Twist ends of strips in opposite directions; place on ungreased baking sheet, pressing ends onto baking sheet to fasten securely. Brush generously with butter; sprinkle with Parmesan cheese. Bake at 425 degrees for 10 to 12 minutes, until golden. Serve with spaghetti sauce for dipping. Makes about 28.

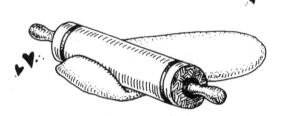

The best way to clean drip pans and reflector bowls from the stove is to take them outside and place on several sheets of newspaper. Give them a heavy coating of oven spray, let sit one hour, then rinse well.

Pizza & Pasta... PRONTO!

Perfect Pasta Salad

Debbie Roberts
Columbus, IN

Toss in any of your favorite veggies...you can't go wrong!

16-oz. pkg. rotini pasta, cooked
1/4 lb. Genoa salami, cubed
1/4 lb. provolone cheese, cubed
1/4 c. celery, diced
1/4 c. carrot, peeled and grated
1 red onion, chopped

2-1/4 oz. can sliced black olives, drained
1/4 c. red or green pepper, chopped
8-oz. pkg. sliced mushrooms

Combine all ingredients in a large serving bowl. Add hot dressing; mix until well blended. Let cool slightly. Serve warm or cold. Serves 8.

Dressing:

3/4 c. white vinegar
3/4 c. sugar
1 c. canola oil

1/2 T. dried basil
1/2 T. dried parsley
1/2 T. dried oregano

Combine all ingredients in a small saucepan over medium heat; cook and stir until hot.

Help banish germs in your kitchen sponge by microwaving for 30 seconds on high setting...simple!

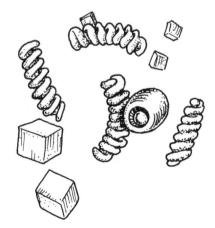

Herbal Garlic Spaghetti

Andrea Vernon
Logansport, IN

Add cooked chicken or shrimp for a heartier meal.

10-oz. pkg. grape tomatoes,
   quartered
1/2 c. olive oil
1/2 c. red wine vinegar
1 onion, diced
2 cloves garlic, minced
1 t. salt

1/2 t. dried basil
1/2 t. dried oregano
1/2 t. pepper
Optional: 1 zucchini, diced
16-oz. pkg. spaghetti, uncooked
Garnish: grated Parmesan
   cheese

Combine first 10 ingredients together in a large serving bowl; set aside. Cook pasta according to package directions, reserving 1/2 cup pasta water. Arrange pasta over tomato mixture; add reserved pasta water. Allow to sit for 2 minutes; toss gently to combine. Garnish with Parmesan cheese. Serves 4 to 6.

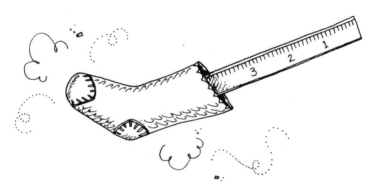

Remove dust bunnies by covering a yardstick with an old sock and slipping it underneath the refrigerator or stove!

Pizza & Pasta... PRONTO!

Creamy Chicken Italiano

Jenny Flake
Gilbert, AZ

This no-fuss dinner is guaranteed to please the entire family.

2 16-oz. jars Alfredo sauce
15-oz. can mixed vegetables,
   drained
12-oz. can chicken, drained
1/2 t. Italian seasoning

1/2 t. salt
1/4 t. pepper
1/4 t. hot pepper sauce
16-oz. pkg. rotini pasta, cooked
1 c. shredded mozzarella cheese

Combine Alfredo sauce, mixed vegetables, chicken, Italian seasoning, salt, pepper and hot pepper sauce in a large saucepan over medium heat. Mix well; simmer for 5 minutes. Add rotini to Alfredo mixture; toss to coat. Reduce heat to low. Sprinkle rotini with cheese; heat until cheese is melted. Serves 6.

An old-fashioned remedy that still works for cleaning copper pots is to sprinkle salt on half a lemon and rub the pot. Rinse and wash with hot soapy water and dry well.

Greek Pizza

Sean Avner
Delaware, OH

*Don't let the anchovies keep you from
trying this...they're completely optional!*

13.8-oz. tube refrigerated pizza
  dough
1/4 c. all-purpose flour
1 to 2 T. olive oil
2 cloves garlic, minced
8-oz. pkg. shredded mozzarella
  cheese, divided
1/2 c. canned artichokes,
  drained and chopped

1/4 c. sliced green olives
3 T. capers
1/2 c. fresh basil, thinly sliced
1/4 c. crumbled feta cheese
Optional: 6 anchovy fillets,
  finely chopped

Roll out pizza dough on a floured surface to about 1/4-inch thick.
Place on a lightly greased baking sheet; brush lightly with olive oil.
Spread garlic over pizza; sprinkle with half the mozzarella. Top with
artichokes, olives, capers, basil, feta and anchovies, if using. Sprinkle
with remaining mozzarella. Bake at 400 degrees for 8 to 10 minutes,
or until cheese melts. Serves 4.

If pasta becomes stuck to a pan, sprinkle some baking soda and
water on the spot and leave overnight. In the morning, use a
plastic scrubbing pad to easily finish up cleaning.

Pizza & Pasta... PRONTO!

Meat & Cheese Stromboli

Kristin DeBusk
Davis, CA

Add a sprinkling of red pepper flakes for extra zing.

16-oz. loaf frozen bread dough,
   thawed and halved
1/4 c. cooked ham, chopped
1/4 c. Canadian bacon, chopped
1/4 c. pepperoni, chopped
1/4 c. sliced black olives
1/4 c. onion, chopped
1/4 c. sliced mushrooms
pepper to taste
8-oz. pkg. shredded mozzarella
   cheese
26-oz. jar spaghetti sauce

Pat one-half of dough onto a lightly greased 15"x10" jelly-roll pan.
Arrange half of all the ingredients except sauce down the center of
dough. Bring each long edge of dough to the center; press together to
seal. Repeat with remaining dough and ingredients on a second lightly
greased jelly-roll pan. Bake at 375 degrees for 20 minutes, or until
lightly golden. Slice and serve with spaghetti sauce. Serves 12.

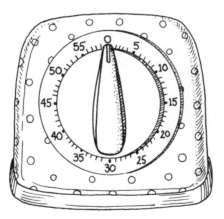

Using slow-cooker liners or oven bags makes quick work
of any after-dinner clean up!

Artichoke-Feta Pasta

Linda Lohmeyer
Kensington, CT

Yummy...that says it all!

2 T. olive oil
6-oz. jar marinated artichokes,
　　drained and quartered
1 clove garlic, minced

6-oz. pkg. crumbled feta cheese
8-oz. pkg. rotini pasta, cooked
1/2 c. pine nuts, toasted
Optional: fresh parsley sprigs

Heat olive oil over medium heat in a large skillet; add artichokes and sauté until slightly softened. Stir in garlic and feta; cook for one minute, or until garlic is lightly golden. Add pasta and pine nuts to artichoke mixture; heat through. Garnish with parsley sprigs, if desired. Serves 3 to 4.

When you drain pasta in a sink, remember to balance the strainer over the sink rather than placing it in the bottom of the sink where there might be soap suds!

Pizza & Pasta... PRONTO!

Sensational Shrimp Linguine

Felice Jones
Boise, ID

This is a recipe I know I can count on. I always prepare it when company's coming!

1 lb. medium shrimp, peeled and
    cleaned
2 roma tomatoes, chopped
3 T. soy sauce
1/4 c. olive oil

1 bunch green onions, chopped
1/4 t. salt-free herb seasoning
16-oz. pkg. linguine pasta,
    cooked
8-oz. container basil pesto

In a large skillet, combine shrimp, tomatoes, soy sauce, olive oil, green onions and seasoning over medium heat. Simmer until shrimp turn pink and tomatoes are soft, about 5 to 8 minutes. Toss with cooked linguine; stir in pesto. Serves 6 to 8.

If dishes have been sitting in the dishwasher for awhile, sprinkle 1/4 cup of baking soda on the bottom of the dishwasher. This will take away any odors from both the dishes and dishwasher.

Buttery Garlic Bread

Marlene Darnell
Newport Beach, CA

A "must-have" with any pasta dish!

1/2 c. butter, softened
2 T. mayonnaise
3 cloves garlic, chopped
2 t. dried oregano
1/4 t. dried sage

1 t. salt
1 t. pepper
1 loaf French bread, halved
   lengthwise
2 T. grated Parmesan cheese

Combine butter, mayonnaise, garlic, herbs, salt and pepper in a medium bowl. Spread mixture evenly on cut surfaces of bread; sprinkle with Parmesan cheese. Broil bread for 5 minutes, or until lightly toasted. Serves 6.

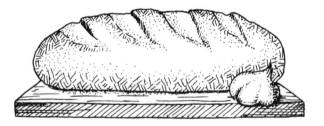

Pour herbs and spices into your hand when adding them to a dish. Sprinkling herbs right from the container over hot food causes them to absorb steam and clump.

Pizza & Pasta... PRONTO!

Everyone's Favorite Salad

Regina Kostyu
Gooseberry Patch

A winning combination of flavors!

1 head iceberg lettuce, torn
4 c. baby spinach
14-oz. can bean sprouts, drained
8 slices bacon, crisply cooked
    and crumbled

Garnish: 3 eggs, hard-boiled,
    peeled and sliced

In a large serving bowl, toss together all ingredients except eggs.
Drizzle dressing over salad. Garnish with egg slices. Serves 6 to 8.

Dressing:

1/2 c. oil
3/4 c. sugar
1/3 c. catsup

1/4 c. vinegar
1 T. Worcestershire sauce
1 onion, chopped

Whisk together all ingredients in a small bowl.

When boiling eggs, add a few
drops of food coloring and
vinegar to the water. The next
time you look
in the fridge, you'll know
exactly which eggs
are hard-boiled!

Buffalo Chicken Pizza

Kris Coburn
Dansville, NY

*There is a difference between "regular" hot pepper sauce
and cayenne pepper sauce. Use the cayenne to get the full flavor.*

12-inch Italian pizza crust	2 c. cooked chicken, diced
1/4 c. butter, melted	1/2 c. celery, chopped
1/4 c. hot cayenne pepper sauce	4-oz. pkg. crumbled blue cheese

Place pizza crust on a lightly greased 12" pizza pan; set aside.
Combine butter and cayenne pepper sauce; mix well. Add chicken and
celery, tossing to coat. Spread chicken mixture evenly over pizza crust.
Sprinkle with blue cheese. Bake at 450 degrees for 10 to 12 minutes,
or until heated through and crust is crisp. Serves 4 to 6.

If your pizza sticks to a pizza baking stone, try this trick.
Use a length of dental floss, longer than the pizza is wide,
and slide it under the pizza.

Pizza & Pasta... PRONTO!

Barbecue Chicken Pizza

Ginny Bone
Saint Peters, MO

When you need dinner fast, keep this quick favorite in mind.

12-inch Italian pizza crust
3 c. cooked chicken, shredded
1 c. barbecue sauce

1 c. shredded mozzarella cheese
1/2 c. shredded Cheddar cheese

Place pizza crust on a lightly greased 12" pizza pan; set aside.
Combine chicken and barbecue sauce; spread on pizza crust. Sprinkle
with cheeses. Bake at 450 degrees for 8 to 10 minutes, or until
cheeses melt and crust is crisp. Serves 4.

Pizza crust gets nice and crispy when baked in a cast-iron
skillet. Season the skillet by giving it a light coat of oil,
then leaving in a 350-degree oven for one hour. Turn the oven
off, but do not open. Allow the skillet to cool down for
several hours, then use paper towels or a coffee filter
to wipe dry before storing.

Tuscan Salad

Helen Eads
Memphis, TN

*One of my favorite recipes. It reminds me of the trip to Italy
my husband and I took...the food was so amazing!
I hope you enjoy this salad as much as we do.*

1 lb. red and yellow tomatoes,
    sliced 1/4-inch thick
1 red onion, diced
4 oranges, peeled and diced

16-oz. pkg. fresh mozzarella
    cheese, diced
1 bunch fresh basil, thinly sliced
salt and pepper to taste

Combine all ingredients in a large salad bowl; add vinaigrette dressing.
Toss gently to coat; serve at room temperature. Serves 6 to 8.

Vinaigrette Dressing:

1/4 c. olive oil
1 T. balsamic vinegar
1 T. sugar

1/4 t. Dijon mustard
1/4 t. salt
1/4 t. garlic, minced

Combine all ingredients in a blender; mix on high setting for
2 minutes.

To keep salad fixin's in a crisper that's extra clean,
wash the crisper drawers with one part bleach to
4 parts water. Rinse and dry well.

Pizza & Pasta... PRONTO!

Traditional Italian Bruschetta

Cathy Hillier
Salt Lake City, UT

Experiment! Bruschetta can be topped with any savory combination of vegetables, fruits or cheese.

4 tomatoes, diced	1 t. fresh basil, chopped
3 T. olive oil	10 slices Italian bread

Combine tomatoes, 2-1/2 teaspoons olive oil and basil; stir until thoroughly combined and set aside. Arrange bread slices in a single layer on an ungreased baking sheet; brush with remaining olive oil. Place bread under broiler until lightly golden, about one minute. Remove from broiler; top with tomato mixture. Serves 10.

Give slices of bruschetta some zip by using flavored olive oils.
Check the grocer for garlic, chili pepper, basil
or even black truffle flavored oils!

Ravioli with Garden Sauce

Susan Copsey-Pearce
Gooseberry Patch

Garlicky flavor with rich broth make this tortellini irresistible.
This is an easy dish for a potluck.

1 clove garlic, minced
1 T. oil
14-1/2 oz. can roasted vegetable
   and herb-flavored chicken
   broth
2 zucchini, sliced
2 c. broccoli flowerets
2 carrots, peeled and sliced into
   thin strips

1 onion, sliced into thin wedges
6-oz. can tomato paste
1/2 t. salt
1/4 t. pepper
25-oz. pkg. frozen ravioli,
   cooked
Garnish: grated Parmesan
   cheese

In a large saucepan, sauté garlic in oil over medium heat until tender.
Add remaining ingredients except ravioli and Parmesan cheese.
Simmer, uncovered, for 10 minutes, or until vegetables are tender.
Serve sauce over prepared ravioli; sprinkle with Parmesan cheese.
Serves 4 to 6.

To peel garlic easily, crush the clove with the side of a knife.
For really speedy mincing, use a garlic press.

Pizza & Pasta... PRONTO!

Smoked Sausage Primavera

Kathy Joy
Covington, TN

Everyone will ask for seconds when you serve this meal!

2 T. butter
1 onion, thinly sliced
1 green pepper, thinly sliced
4-oz. can sliced mushrooms,
    drained

1 lb. smoked sausage, cut into
    bite-size pieces
16-oz. pkg. spaghetti, cooked
2 T. olive oil
1/4 c. grated Parmesan cheese

Melt butter over medium heat in a large non-stick skillet. Add onion and green pepper; sauté until almost translucent. Add mushrooms; cook for one to 2 minutes longer, or until mushrooms are heated through. Remove vegetables and set aside. Add sausage to skillet and cook just until it begins to brown, 3 to 4 minutes; drain. Return vegetables to skillet; toss to combine and set aside. Toss cooked spaghetti with oil. To serve, place spaghetti in the center of a serving platter. Top with sausage mixture; sprinkle with Parmesan cheese just before serving. Serves 6 to 8.

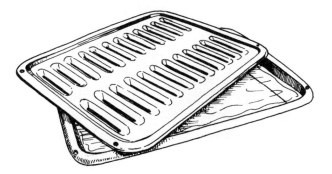

To make clean-up easier when using the broiler, put a little water in the pan beneath the broiling rack. The water not only makes it easier to clean the pan, but also absorbs any smoke.

Linguine with Clams

Elizabeth Cisneros
Chino Hills, CA

I like to top servings with freshly cracked black pepper.

1/2 c. butter
1/2 c. olive oil
8 cloves garlic, minced
2 10-oz. cans baby clams,
    drained and liquid reserved
2 c. white wine or clam juice

1/4 c. fresh parsley, minced
8-oz. pkg. linguine pasta,
    cooked
pepper to taste

Melt butter and oil together in a large skillet over medium heat; add garlic and sauté until tender. Add reserved clam liquid and wine or clam juice; reduce heat and simmer for 10 minutes. Stir in clams and parsley; simmer for an additional 5 minutes. Toss pasta with clam mixture; sprinkle with pepper. Serve immediately. Serves 4.

Eggshells are so helpful for cleaning glass bottles! Break clean shells into pieces and drop them into the bottle with a few drops of detergent. Add a little water, shake vigorously, and then rinse well with water.

Pizza & Pasta... PRONTO!

Quick & Spicy Shrimp Linguine

Laurel Perry
Loganville, GA

Impress your friends & family with this easy-to-sauté classic recipe.

2 T. butter
2 cloves garlic, minced
14-1/2 oz. can spicy stewed
    tomatoes
1 lb. large shrimp, peeled,
    cleaned and cooked

1 red pepper, diced
2 green onions, chopped
8-oz. pkg. linguine pasta,
    cooked
Garnish: grated Parmesan
    cheese

Melt butter over medium heat in a large skillet. Add garlic; cook until
fragrant, about one minute. Add tomatoes with juice; bring to a boil.
Simmer uncovered, stirring occasionally, for about 10 minutes, or
until slightly thickened. Add shrimp, red pepper and green onions;
cook for about 5 minutes, until shrimp turn pink. Stir in hot pasta; toss
until well coated. Garnish with Parmesan cheese. Serves 4.

Did you know that odors will disappear overnight from plastic
storage containers if you pack them with crumpled newspaper
and secure the lid tightly?

Italian Chicken Pasta Salad

Becky Dunscomb
Forsyth, IL

*Simply tossed with Italian dressing, this recipe is the perfect
answer to a picnic or light supper.*

8-oz. pkg. penne pasta, cooked
2 boneless, skinless chicken
    breasts, cooked and cubed
4 plum tomatoes, chopped

2-1/4 oz. can sliced black olives,
    drained
6-oz. pkg. crumbled feta cheese

Combine all ingredients in a large bowl. Toss with Italian Dressing;
chill. Serves 4.

Italian Dressing:

3/4 c. olive oil
2 T. white wine vinegar
1 t. Italian seasoning

2 t. Dijon mustard
1 t. salt
1 t. pepper

Whisk all ingredients together; chill.

Pasta salads can be mixed with crabmeat, shrimp, tuna or a
variety of fresh vegetables. Divide the salad into individual
bowls and make each one different!

Homestyle Beef Pot Pie

Doris Stegner
Gooseberry Patch

This traditional dish is a meal all by itself.

16-oz. pkg. frozen potato, green
    bean, onion and red pepper
    mixture
2 T. water
1/2 t. dried thyme
12-oz. jar mushroom gravy

1 lb. roast beef, cubed
pepper to taste
8-oz. tube refrigerated
    crescent rolls

Combine vegetables, water and thyme in an oven-proof skillet. Cook
over medium heat until vegetables are thawed, about 3 minutes. Stir
in gravy; bring to a boil. Remove from heat. Add beef; mix well.
Sprinkle with pepper. Separate crescent rolls into 8 triangles. Starting
at wide ends, roll up halfway; arrange over beef mixture so pointed
ends are directed to the center. Bake at 375 degrees for 17 to
19 minutes, or until rolls are golden. Serves 4.

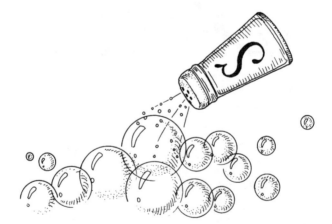

If you find there are too many suds in your dishwater, simply
sprinkle a little salt on them and they will subside in no time!

Dinner in a Dash

Quick Sausage Supper

Melissa Hutchinson
Gallipolis, OH

My favorite way to enjoy this supper...with a crispy salad tossed with balsamic vinaigrette and chocolate pudding for dessert!

1/4 c. olive oil, divided
1 clove garlic, minced
salt and pepper to taste
16-oz. pkg. Kielbasa, sliced
    into 1-inch thick pieces

1/2 c. sweet onion, sliced
1 green pepper, cut into strips
8-oz. pkg. sliced mushrooms
5 redskin potatoes, cooked
    and diced

In a large skillet, heat one tablespoon oil over medium heat; add garlic, salt and pepper. Cook about one minute. Add 2 tablespoons oil and sausage to skillet; sauté over medium heat until golden, about 10 minutes. Drain Kielbasa mixture on paper towels; set aside. Add remaining oil to skillet; sauté onion, pepper and mushrooms until liquid evaporates. Add potatoes and return Kielbasa mixture to skillet; heat through. Makes 4 servings.

Remember that a freshly washed throw rug just taken out of the dryer will have a warm rubber backing. Don't place the rugs on your tile floors right away. The rubber may either discolor the tile or even stick to it because of the heat. Lay the rug rubber-side up until completely cooled.

Crab Rice Cakes

Tina Goodpasture
Meadowview, VA

If you love rice and crab, then this is the recipe for you.
I find it's so simple to make and very good.

1 c. chicken broth
1 c. instant rice, uncooked
2 eggs

2 6-oz. cans crabmeat, drained
1/4 c. grated Parmesan cheese
1/4 c. butter

Bring chicken broth to a boil in a small saucepan over medium-high heat. Stir in rice; cover. Remove from heat and let stand 5 minutes. Fluff rice with a fork; set aside. Beat eggs in a medium bowl. Add rice, crabmeat and cheese; mix well. Shape mixture into 8 patties. Let stand for 5 minutes. Melt butter in a large skillet over medium heat. Add patties; cook about 5 minutes per side, or until golden and heated through. Serves 4.

Save recipe prep time by picking up a carton of beaten eggs
in the dairy department. Great for dinner recipes,
but also makes quick work of scrambled eggs for breakfast!

DiNNER in a Dash

Mom's Tuna Pie

Cam Scott
Aurora, IN

You can place a pastry crust on top if you'd like.
Just flute the crust edges and vent before baking.

2 eggs, beaten
1/2 c. milk
1 T. butter, melted
1/4 c. onion, chopped

3/4 t. dried basil
1/4 t. salt
2 6-oz. cans tuna, drained

Combine all ingredients together in a medium bowl; spread mixture into a greased 8" pie plate. Bake at 425 degrees for 25 minutes. Serves 4 to 6.

Salmon Patties

Caroline Payne
Monticello, MO

Replace the salmon with canned tuna if that's what you have in the pantry, or do a combination of tuna and salmon!

14-3/4 oz. can salmon,
    drained
1 egg, beaten
1/3 c. dry bread crumbs

1 t. onion, minced
1/4 t. salt
1/4 t. dried thyme
1/8 t. pepper

Mix all ingredients together in a medium bowl until well blended. Shape into 3 patties; arrange in a lightly greased 8"x8" baking pan. Bake at 375 degrees for 20 to 25 minutes, or until firm. Serves 3.

To clean a thermos, fill it with water, drop in 4 denture cleaning tablets, and let soak for an hour.

Nachos for a Crowd

Colleen Seaton
Nashville, IL

A great way to use leftover chili!

13-1/2 oz. bag round tortilla
  chips
15-oz. can homestyle chili
8-oz. pkg. shredded Mexican-
  blend cheese
1/2 c. queso sauce
10-oz. pkg. shredded lettuce
1 onion, diced

1 green pepper, chopped
1/2 c. jalapeño pepper, sliced
Optional: 1/2 c. sliced black
  olives, 4-oz. can diced green
  chiles
1/2 c. sour cream
1 tomato, diced
2 T. dried chives

Arrange chips on a large microwave-safe plate; set aside. Heat chili in a microwave-safe bowl on high setting for one minute; stir. Microwave for another minute; set aside. Sprinkle tortilla chips with cheese; microwave on high setting for 30 seconds. Spoon chili and queso sauce over cheese; sprinkle with lettuce, onion, green pepper and jalapeño. Top with black olives and green chiles, if using. Add a dollop of sour cream; sprinkle with tomato and chives. Serves 6 to 8.

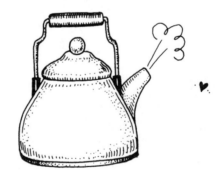

It's easy to remove the hard water and lime build-up in a teakettle. Pour in 2 cups of white vinegar and bring to a boil. Let simmer for about 10 minutes, then rinse well.

Dinner in a Dash

Mexicali Bean Salad

Lorrie Williamson
Maple Valley, WA

We also like to toss in cooked shrimp for a special treat!

16-oz. can pinto beans, drained
  and rinsed
16-oz. kidney beans, drained
  and rinsed
16-oz. can black beans, drained
  and rinsed
16-oz. can Great Northern
  beans, drained and rinsed

15-oz. can corn, drained
6-oz. can black olives, drained
2 tomatoes, chopped
1 c. red onion, chopped
1 bunch fresh cilantro, chopped
16-oz. bottle Italian salad
  dressing
2 limes

Combine beans and corn in a large bowl. Add olives, tomatoes, onion, cilantro and salad dressing; mix well. Squeeze the juice of one lime over salad, mixing well. Slice remaining lime and arrange around edge of salad. Serves 10 to 12.

Your blenders and food processors can practically clean themselves! Filled with warm water and 2 drops of dishwashing liquid, just cover and run at low speed. Empty, fill with clear water and run again to rinse thoroughly.

Broccoli-Cheese Soup

Nichole Martelli
Alvin, TX

A favorite comfort food.

10-3/4 oz. can cream of celery
    soup
10-3/4 oz. can Cheddar cheese
    soup
1-1/4 c. milk
1/4 t. garlic powder

1/4 t. onion powder
1/8 t. pepper
1 c. shredded Cheddar cheese
2 to 3 c. broccoli, chopped
    and cooked

Combine soups, milk, garlic powder, onion powder and pepper in a saucepan. Cook over medium heat until hot, stirring occasionally. Add cheese; stir until melted. Add broccoli and continue to stir over low heat until soup is heated through. Serves 4 to 6.

Grind up a cup of rice in a coffee grinder...it not only cleans
the grinder, but sharpens the blades too!

Dinner in a Dash

Eva's Potatoes

Lora Sargent
Bonney Lake, WA

All I can say is...delicious!

8-oz. pkg. shredded sharp
   Cheddar cheese
1/4 c. butter
1/3 c. green onion, chopped
6 potatoes, peeled, cooked
   and cubed

2 c. sour cream
1 t. salt
1/4 t. pepper

Combine cheese and butter in a saucepan; cook over low heat until almost melted. Remove from heat; spoon into a lightly greased 13"x9" baking pan. Stir in onion, potatoes and sour cream; sprinkle with salt and pepper. Bake at 350 degrees for 20 minutes. Serves 6 to 8.

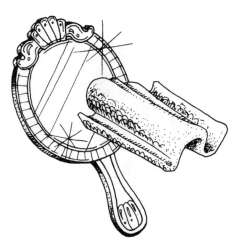

For streak-free mirrors, clean them with rubbing alcohol and a soft cotton cloth.

Mushroom-Chicken Bake

Debbie Rieder
Crimora, VA

*If you preheat the oven while you are doing the prep work, your oven
waits for you, instead of you waiting on the oven!*

10-3/4 oz. can cream of
  mushroom soup
1/2 c. sour cream
1/2 c. cottage cheese
8-oz. can mushroom stems
  and pieces, drained

6-oz. can chicken, drained
8-oz. pkg. penne pasta, cooked
14-oz. pkg. frozen chopped
  broccoli

Combine soup, sour cream and cottage cheese in a large bowl; mix
well. Fold in mushrooms, chicken and cooked pasta. Spread in a
lightly greased 3-quart casserole dish. Top with frozen broccoli; cover
and bake at 350 degrees for 25 to 30 minutes. Serves 6.

Did you know that if you store your cottage cheese or
sour cream cartons upside-down the contents will stay fresher
longer? Storing cartons this way prevents air from getting
inside which means a much better taste!

DiNNER in a Dash

Ham Tetrazzini

Amy Allen
Monticello, IN

Rich and creamy and elegant enough for company.

10-3/4 oz. can cream of
   mushroom soup
1/2 c. milk
1-1/2 c. shredded Cheddar
   cheese

1-lb. pkg. cooked ham, cubed
6-oz. pkg. spaghetti, cooked
salt and pepper

Combine soup, milk and cheese in a large skillet over medium heat. Cook until cheese is melted, stirring often. Add ham and cooked spaghetti; heat through. Add salt and pepper to taste. Serves 4 to 6.

If you drop an egg on the floor, cover it with salt,
wait 5 minutes and it will easily sweep up!

Taco-Rice Skillet

Jamie Bowser
Holton, KS

Use hot salsa and Pepper Jack cheese for real zing!

1 lb. ground beef, browned
    and drained
16-oz. jar salsa
8-oz. can tomato sauce

1 c. instant rice, cooked
Garnish: shredded Cheddar
    cheese, sour cream and
    tortilla chips

Combine beef, salsa and tomato sauce in a saucepan over medium heat; heat through. Serve over rice garnished with cheese, sour cream and tortilla chips. Serves 4.

Crispy-Crunchy Burritos

Lois Bivens
Gooseberry Patch

The tortilla is so crispy on the outside, while still soft inside.

4 6-inch corn or flour tortillas
2 T. cooked beef or pork,
    shredded
2 T. refried beans, warmed

2 T. salsa
2 T. shredded Monterey Jack
    cheese
2 T. sour cream

Place 2 tortillas in a large skillet that has been lightly sprayed with non-stick vegetable spray. Top each tortilla with one tablespoon each of remaining ingredients; top with remaining tortilla. Cook over medium heat until golden; flip and continue to cook until golden and cheese is melted. Serves 2.

Rubbing alcohol is an excellent cleaner for removing ballpoint pen marks from a painted wall!

DiNNER in a Dash

Salsa Beef & Mac

Tammy Steinert
Hoisington, KS

When I'm in a hurry, I make this dish. It's easy and I always have the ingredients on hand.

1/2 lb. ground beef
7-1/4 oz. pkg. macaroni
   & cheese

1/2 c. salsa

Brown beef in a skillet over medium heat; drain and set aside. Prepare macaroni and cheese according to package directions; add to beef. Stir in salsa; heat through, about 2 to 3 minutes over medium heat. Serves 4.

Oodles of Noodles Chili Bake

Robin Kessler
Fresno, CA

If you want, create a different dish by adding your favorite vegetables. It is delicious either way and foolproof.

1 lb. ground beef, browned
   and drained
15-oz. can chili
1 c. shredded Cheddar cheese,
   divided

14-1/2 oz. can diced tomatoes
15-oz. can corn, drained
12-oz. pkg. egg noodles, cooked

Mix beef, chili, 3/4 cup cheese, tomatoes, corn and noodles together in a lightly greased 13"x9" baking pan; sprinkle with remaining cheese. Bake at 350 degrees until heated through, about 20 minutes. Serves 4.

It's easy to remove baked-on food from a stovetop...just cover the spots with equal parts water and baking soda and let the food soak right off.

Quick Homemade Pasta Sauce

Jami Steiger
Medina, OH

*Excellent for spaghetti, eggplant parmigiana, lasagna or pizza
and it also freezes well.*

1 lb. ground beef, browned
   and drained
2 29-oz. cans tomato sauce
1/4 c. tomato paste
1/4 c. balsamic vinegar
2 t. olive oil
2 T. sugar

2 T. dried parsley
2 t. dried basil
1 t. Italian seasoning
1 T. plus 1 t. onion powder
1 T. plus 1 t. garlic, minced
1/2 t. pepper

Mix together all ingredients in a large saucepan; bring to a boil over
medium-high heat. Reduce heat to medium; simmer uncovered,
stirring occasionally, for about 15 minutes. Serves 6.

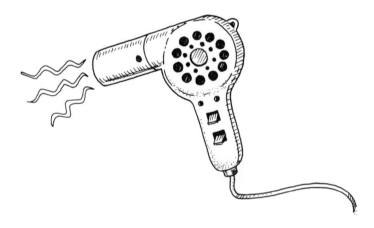

To remove pesky price tag stickers, run a hot hair dryer over
the sticker for 30 seconds and peel off. You can also rub the
sticker with a soft cloth dampened with alcohol.

Dinner in a Dash

Baked Broccoli & Cheese

Katherine Lawler
Rochester, NY

This version is a little bit richer and a little bit cheesier than other casserole recipes, but still a snap to make.

10-oz. pkg. frozen broccoli, thawed
12-oz. pkg. shredded Cheddar cheese

16-oz. container sour cream
1.8-oz. pkg. vegetable soup mix, divided

Combine all ingredients except soup mix. Sprinkle one envelope vegetable soup mix over broccoli mixture. Reserve second envelope for another recipe. Pour broccoli mixture into a lightly greased 2-quart casserole dish. Bake at 350 degrees for 25 to 30 minutes, or until heated through. Serves 6.

Tickle the ivories with a mixture of salt and lemon juice...ideal for cleaning piano keys.

3-Bean Delight

Jennifer Dartlon
Oak Grove, LA

You can also use ground beef in place of ground sausage.

1 lb. breakfast link sausage, sliced
1 lb. ground pork sausage
1 onion, chopped
16-oz. can kidney beans, drained and rinsed
16-oz. can Great Northern beans, drained and rinsed
16-oz. can pinto beans with jalapeños, drained and rinsed
10-3/4 oz. can cream of chicken soup
10-oz. can tomatoes with chiles

Sauté sausages and onion in a large saucepan over medium heat for 10 minutes, or until sausages are no longer pink; drain. Add remaining ingredients; simmer for 15 minutes. Serves 10 to 12.

Crayon masterpieces on the wall? Sprinkle baking soda on a damp sponge and rub the crayon right off!

DiNNER in a Dash

Corned Beef Casserole

Sophia Graves
Okeechobee, FL

My mom always made this favorite casserole on Wednesday nights. Since we had church meetings that night, she wanted to get dinner prepared quickly. I later discovered the recipe was handed down from my dad's mom...she also always made it on Wednesday nights!

8-oz. pkg. elbow macaroni,
   cooked
10-3/4 oz. can cream of
   mushroom soup
12-oz. can corned beef, cubed
1/2 c. onion, diced
salt and pepper to taste
8-oz. pkg. shredded Swiss
   cheese

Combine all ingredients except cheese; pour into a greased 2-quart casserole dish. Sprinkle cheese over top. Bake at 350 degrees until cheese melts and starts to turn golden, about 20 minutes. Serves 4.

One-Pot Dinner

Crystal Hamlett
Amory, MS

I make this dinner when the day's been filled with errands.

1 lb. smoked sausage, sliced
1 head cabbage, cut into chunks
28-oz. can Italian green beans,
   drained
2 14-1/2 oz. cans sliced new
   potatoes, drained
1 onion, sliced
salt and pepper to taste
1/2 c. butter
1/2 to 1 c. water

In a large pot, layer sausage, cabbage, beans, potatoes and onion. Sprinkle with salt and pepper. Slice butter over top; add water. Cover and cook over medium-high heat for 5 minutes, or until cabbage begins to wilt. Reduce heat and cook until done, about 10 minutes. Serves 4.

Beefy Rice Fiesta

Brandi Ciccarella
Bent Mountain, VA

*A tried & true dish my grandmother made quite often
when I was growing up.*

1 lb. ground beef
1/4 c. onion, chopped
1 T. oil
15-oz. can corn, drained
14-1/2 oz. can whole tomatoes
1 green pepper, chopped

1 t. chili powder
2 t. salt
1/4 t. pepper
1-1/2 c. water
1 cube beef bouillon
1-1/2 c. instant rice, uncooked

Combine beef, onion and oil in a large skillet. Cook over medium heat
until ground beef is browned. Drain and stir in vegetables, chili
powder, salt and pepper; simmer for 10 to 15 minutes. Meanwhile,
bring water to a boil; dissolve bouillon. Add to ground beef mixture;
stir in rice. Simmer for 5 to 8 minutes, or until rice is cooked.
Serves 6 to 8.

Bouillon granules are quick-dissolving for use in any
recipe...keep a jar in your pantry!

Dinner in a Dash

Mediterranean Roast Chicken

Karen Pilcher
Burleson, TX

*Rotisserie chicken from the grocer is tender and
ideal in this time-saving recipe.*

14-1/2 oz. can diced tomatoes
   with roasted garlic and
   onions
6-oz. jar quartered artichokes,
   drained

1/3 c. pitted Kalamata olives
3 to 4-lb. deli roast chicken
1/2 c. crumbled feta cheese

Combine tomatoes, artichokes and olives in a small saucepan over
medium heat; bring to a boil. Simmer for one minute. Spoon sauce
over chicken; sprinkle with feta cheese. Serves 6.

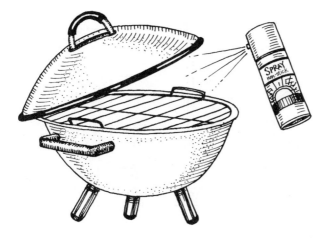

Shorten grill clean-up time by spraying the rack with non-stick
vegetable spray before using.

Best-Ever Pasta Alfredo

Tiffany Brinkley
Broomfield, CO

Mmm, pasta covered with a velvety Alfredo sauce.

1 c. whipping cream
1/4 c. butter

3/4 c. grated Parmesan cheese
cooked pasta

Combine ingredients except pasta in a medium saucepan. Cook and stir over medium-low heat until smooth, about 8 to 10 minutes. Remove from heat; let stand to thicken, about 5 minutes. Serve over hot cooked pasta. Makes 4 servings.

No more fog on the bathroom window! The next time
you clean your window, use a mixture of water
with a tiny bit of dish soap in it, then wipe dry.

Dinner in a Dash

Fast Chicken Noodle Soup

Amy Williams
Bolivar, OH

*The addition of ginger makes this
noodle soup stand out from all the rest.*

2 14-1/2 oz. cans chicken broth
5-oz. can chicken, drained
4-oz. can sliced mushrooms,
   drained
2 t. fresh ginger, peeled and
   grated
2 t. soy sauce
2 c. medium egg noodles,
   cooked
1/4 c. green onion, sliced
2 T. fresh cilantro, chopped

Bring broth to a boil over medium-high heat in a 2-quart saucepan.
Reduce heat; stir in chicken, mushrooms, ginger and soy sauce.
Simmer for 3 minutes; stir in noodles, onion and cilantro. Return to a
simmer and heat through. Serves 4.

Stadium Soup

Cam Scott
Aurora, IN

I love this with a thick slice of buttered cornbread.

1-1/2 c. potatoes, peeled
   and diced
1 c. carrots, peeled and sliced
1 c. celery, sliced
1 c. onion, diced
1-1/2 c. cooked ham, cubed
4 c. water
16-oz. pkg. pasteurized process
   cheese spread, cubed
salt and pepper to taste

Combine all ingredients except cheese, salt and
pepper in a large soup pot. Cook over medium
heat for 5 minutes, until vegetables are
tender; add cheese and stir until melted.
Sprinkle with salt and pepper to taste.
Serves 4 to 6.

Fresh Herbed Rice

Cheri Maxwell
Gulf Breeze, FL

Cilantro and green chiles come together to dress up ordinary rice.

1 c. long-cooking rice, uncooked
2 c. chicken broth
4-oz. can diced green chiles
1 onion, diced
1 t. dried oregano

1/2 t. ground cumin
1/2 t. salt
3 green onions, sliced
1/3 c. fresh cilantro, chopped

Combine rice, broth, chiles, onion, oregano, cumin and salt in a large saucepan over medium-high heat; bring to a boil. Reduce heat to low; cover and simmer until liquid is absorbed, about 20 minutes. Stir in green onions and cilantro. Serves 4 to 6.

Erase grease spatters on the wall behind the stove.
Make a thick paste of baking soda and water, apply to the
grease stain and let dry. Wipe clean with a soft cloth.

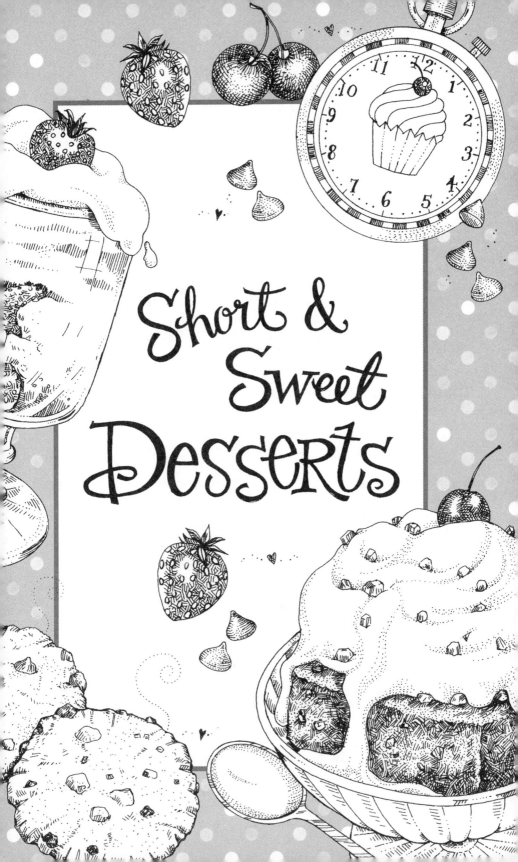

Short & Sweet Desserts

Pound Cake Cobbler   *Vickie*

Enjoy a fruit-filled cobbler in 10 minutes!

12-oz. pkg. pound cake, cubed
21-oz. can cherry pie filling
1/3 c. water

1/2 t. almond extract
2 T. slivered almonds, toasted

Arrange pound cake in a microwave-safe dish; set aside. Combine cherry pie filling, water and almond extract in a small bowl. Spoon over cubed pound cake; sprinkle with almonds. Cover with plastic wrap; microwave on high setting for 5 to 7 minutes, or until filling is bubbly. Serve immediately. Makes 8 servings.

Dandy Candy Apples   *Barbara Pache*
                                    Marshall, WI

The grandkids love this!

3 apples, cored and cut into
    bite-size pieces
2 2.7-oz. caramel-peanut candy
    bars, diced

12-oz. container frozen whipped
    topping, thawed

Combine all ingredients in a medium bowl; refrigerate until ready to serve. Serves 4 to 6.

To clean metal burner rings, fill the sink with hot water and one cup of ammonia. Let the rings soak all night, then rub clean in the morning.

Short & Sweet Desserts

Cinnamon-Apple Parfaits

Courtney Robinson
Gooseberry Patch

A yummy, warm parfait.

1 c. quick-cooking oats, uncooked
1/2 c. brown sugar, packed
1/4 c. butter, melted

21-oz. can apple pie filling
1/4 t. cinnamon
1 qt. vanilla ice cream, slightly softened

Combine oats, brown sugar and butter; spread into an ungreased 8"x8" baking pan. Bake at 350 degrees for 10 minutes. Cool, crumble and set aside. In a medium bowl, mix together pie filling and cinnamon; divide mixture among 8 parfait glasses. Top with softened ice cream and crumbled oat mixture. Serves 8.

Quickly soften ice cream in the carton using the microwave on high setting...

one pint = 10 to 15 seconds
one quart = 15 to 25 seconds
1/2 gallon = 30 to 40 seconds

Cream Cheese Apple Dip

Staci Meyers
Cocoa, FL

You won't be able to stop dipping into this creamy concoction!

8-oz. pkg. cream cheese,
    softened
1/4 c. sugar
3/4 c. brown sugar, packed

1 t. vanilla extract
1/2 c. toffee baking bits
marshmallows, pretzels and
    apple slices

Blend together cream cheese and sugars; mix in vanilla. Stir in toffee bits. Serve at room temperature with marshmallows, pretzels and apple slices. Makes about 2 cups.

You probably know that lemon juice keeps
apple slices from browning, but did you know that
lemon-lime soda works just as well?

Short & Sweet Desserts

Strawberry Angel Dessert

Lynda Robson
Boston, MA

*This sweet treat serves 12 to 14, making it
ideal for a family reunion or carry-in.*

10-inch angel food cake
2 8-oz. pkgs. cream cheese,
  softened
1 c. sugar
8-oz. container frozen whipped
  topping, thawed

1 qt. strawberries, hulled and
  sliced
18-oz. jar strawberry glaze

Crumble cake into an ungreased 13"x9" baking pan; set aside.
Combine cream cheese and sugar; mix until light and fluffy. Fold in
whipped topping. Press cake down with hands; spread cream cheese
mixture over top. In a small bowl, combine strawberries and glaze
until berries are evenly coated; spread over cream cheese layer. Chill
until ready to serve. Serves 12 to 14.

To easily clean strawberries, place them in a sink of water
and gently wash with the sprayer nozzle on the sink.
The water from the nozzle will toss and turn the
strawberries, giving them a thorough cleaning.

Rocky Road Dessert Cups

Shelley Turner
Boise, ID

All the best flavors of Rocky Road ice cream, but in a pudding!

1-oz. pkg. instant chocolate
   pudding mix
2 c. milk

1-1/2 c. mini marshmallows
1/2 c. dry-roasted peanuts,
   chopped

Prepare pudding with milk according to package directions. Fold in marshmallows and peanuts; spoon into 4 individual cups and chill until set. Makes 4 servings.

English Toffee Chocolate Trifle

J.J. Presley
Portland, TX

A glass serving dish is a must to show off all the yummy layers!

18-1/2 oz. devil's food
   chocolate cake mix
24-oz. bottle chocolate syrup

8-oz. pkg. toffee baking bits
16-oz. container frozen whipped
   topping, thawed

Bake cake according to package directions; cool and crumble. In a large glass bowl, layer one-third each starting with cake, chocolate syrup, toffee bits and whipped topping. Repeat layers 2 more times. Chill and serve. Makes 6 to 8 servings.

To give appliances a sweet smell, wash the outsides with warm water that you've dropped one teaspoon of vanilla extract into!

Butter Pecan Mousse

Rhonda Reeder
Ellicott City, MD

Garnish servings with additional pecans if you'd like.

3/4 c. chopped pecans
1 T. butter, melted
2 8-oz. pkgs. cream cheese,
   softened

1/4 c. sugar
1/4 c. brown sugar, packed
1/2 t. vanilla extract
1 c. whipping cream, whipped

Combine pecans and butter; spread on an ungreased baking sheet. Bake at 350 degrees for 5 minutes, or until lightly toasted; cool. Finely chop; set aside. Beat cream cheese at medium speed with an electric mixer until smooth. Add sugars and vanilla, mixing well. Stir in toasted pecans; gently fold in whipped cream. Spoon into serving dishes; chill until ready to serve. Serves 6.

Dessert in a dash...cube cake and layer in a parfait cup along with vanilla yogurt. Top with a cherry!

Sugar Cream Pie

Carol Lanham
Woodstock, OH

Not only can this pie be made in just a few short minutes,
I've never served it to anyone who didn't love it!

1 c. sugar
1/4 c. cornstarch
1-1/4 c. evaporated milk
1 c. milk

1/2 c. butter, sliced
9-inch pie crust, baked
Garnish: cinnamon

Mix together all ingredients except pie crust and cinnamon in a large saucepan. Cook over low heat until mixture thickens, stirring constantly. Pour into pie crust; sprinkle with cinnamon and let cool. Refrigerate until ready to serve. Serves 6.

If you find your purchased graham cracker or chocolate cookie crust has a small crack in it, simply invert the plastic lid and place it over the crust. Gently rubbing over the crack with your finger will help bring the crust back together.

Short & Sweet Desserts

Tropical Fruit Whip

Connie Bryant
Topeka, KS

*Sprinkle servings with flaked coconut and tuck in
a mini paper umbrella for a whimsical dessert!*

3-1/2 oz. pkg. instant vanilla
    pudding mix
15-1/4 oz. can crushed
    pineapple

1-1/2 to 2 c. mini marshmallows
15-oz. can fruit cocktail, drained
8-oz. container frozen whipped
    topping, thawed

Mix together pudding and crushed pineapple with juice. Add remaining
ingredients; mix well. Chill until ready to serve. Serves 8 to 10.

Be sure to treat tablecloth stains as soon as possible. For the
best results, soak the fabric in cold water for 5 to 10 minutes,
then rub detergent into the stained area and launder as usual.

Coconut Cake Bars

Lisa Langston
Conroe, TX

Sure to be a hit at the next bake sale!

12-oz. pkg. pound cake mix
1/2 c. butter, softened
1 c. honey

14-oz. pkg. sweetened flaked
coconut

Slice cake 1-1/2 inches thick; cut each slice into 4 strips. Spread butter and honey on 3 sides of cake strips; roll in coconut to coat. Arrange strips on a greased baking sheet. Bake at 375 degrees for 5 to 10 minutes, just until toasted and golden. Makes about 20.

To easily soften honey that's crystallized, set the jar in a pan of water and heat on the stove over low heat. In no time at all, the honey will be ready to use in any recipe.

Short & Sweet Desserts

Chocolate Chippers

Connie Laxton
Guthrie, OK

How can you miss when you combine chocolate chips and peanut butter?

1 c. creamy or crunchy
   peanut butter
1 c. sugar
1 egg, beaten
1/2 c. semi-sweet chocolate
   chips

1/2 c. quick-cooking oats,
   uncooked
1 t. vanilla extract

Combine all ingredients; mix well. Drop by teaspoonfuls onto ungreased baking sheets. Bake at 350 degrees for 15 minutes; cool. Makes 2 dozen.

To remove eggs from mixing bowls, soak bowls in cold water. Hot water will actually cook the egg, making it even harder to remove.

Caramelized Pears

Jo Ann

A rich ending to any meal.

2 pears, cored, peeled and sliced
juice of 1 lemon
2 T. butter

2 T. sugar
1/2 t. cinnamon
8 gingerbread cookies

Toss pears with lemon juice; set aside. Heat butter in a large skillet over medium heat; add pears. Cook, stirring frequently, until butter begins to brown. Sprinkle sugar over pears; stir gently until sugar caramelizes and pears are tender, about 3 to 4 minutes. Remove from heat; sprinkle with cinnamon. Serve warm with gingerbread cookies. Serves 4.

Create chocolate drizzles with little effort!
Thinly slice a chocolate bar and scatter on a warm cake.

Short & Sweet Desserts

Strawberry-Melon Whip

Sasha Kelton
Henrietta, TX

Oh-so refreshing!

1 pt. strawberries, hulled
    and sliced
1 cantaloupe, peeled, seeded
    and sliced
1 to 2 8-oz. containers
    strawberry yogurt
cinnamon to taste

Mix together fruit and yogurt; sprinkle with cinnamon. Serves 2.

Dreamy Banana Pudding

Mary Murray
Gooseberry Patch

*An easy banana pudding recipe, made special with
frozen whipped topping and vanilla wafers.*

3-1/2 oz. pkg. instant vanilla
    pudding mix
2 c. milk
12-oz. pkg. vanilla wafers,
    divided
3 bananas, sliced
8-oz. container frozen whipped
    topping, thawed

Prepare pudding with milk according to package directions; set aside
in refrigerator. Arrange vanilla wafers in a single layer to cover bottom
of an ungreased 8" round cake pan. Reserve any remaining wafers for
another recipe. Pour pudding over wafers. Arrange banana slices on
top of pudding; spread with whipped topping. Serve immediately or
refrigerate. Serves 4.

To speed banana ripening, place them in a
plastic bag. To help them stay fresh longer,
refrigerate them. The peels will darken, but the
bananas will last for about 2 weeks.

Nutty Brownie Pizza

Tanya Graham
Lawrenceville, GA

Ask your local pizza parlor for some new pizza boxes,
then deliver this yummy treat to a special friend!

21-oz. pkg. brownie mix
1-1/2 c. chocolate sandwich
  cookies, crushed
1 c. mini marshmallows
1/4 c. chopped walnuts

1/4 c. candy-coated peanut
  butter candies

Prepare brownie mix batter according to package directions. Stir in cookie crumbs; mix well. Spread mixture in a lightly greased 14" deep-dish pizza pan; bake at 350 degrees for 18 minutes, or until a toothpick inserted into center comes out clean. Sprinkle marshmallows evenly over hot brownies; return to oven for 3 minutes, until marshmallows are lightly golden. Sprinkle with walnuts and peanut butter candies; gently press nuts and candies into marshmallows. Cut into squares and serve warm. Serves 8 to 10.

Toast nuts by pouring one cup into a microwave-safe dish
and heating on the high setting in the microwave.
One to 2 minutes should do it.

Short & Sweet Desserts

Easy-Breezy Caramel Brownies

Brynne Stevenson
Springfield, OH

What more can I tell you...this is wonderful!

21-oz. pkg. brownie mix
16-oz. container milk chocolate
   frosting

6 to 8 T. caramel ice cream
   topping
Optional: chopped nuts

Bake brownies according to package directions; set aside. Mix together frosting and ice cream topping in a microwave-safe bowl. Cook on high setting for 45 seconds; stir and pour over brownies. Top with chopped nuts, if desired. Serves 10 to 12.

Does the kitchen floor have scuff marks? Remove them
with a pencil eraser or dry paper towel!

Banana-Cherry Sponge Cake

Megan Brooks
Antioch, TN

It's easy to use a prepared 6-ounce box of instant vanilla pudding mix instead of a can of pudding.

15-oz. pkg. cream-filled sponge
   cakes
15-3/4 oz. can vanilla pudding
2 bananas, sliced

21-oz. can cherry pie filling
8-oz. container frozen whipped
   topping, thawed

Slice sponge cakes in half lengthwise; arrange in an ungreased 13"x9" baking pan. Layer vanilla pudding, bananas and pie filling over top. Spread whipped topping over pie filling. Chill until ready to serve. Serves 8 to 10.

Chocolate Silk Pie

Amy Butcher
Columbus, GA

Takes just a few minutes to prepare, but plan ahead...this pie needs to chill 3 hours before serving.

3-1/2 oz. pkg. chocolate
   pudding mix
1-3/4 c. milk

9-inch pie crust, baked
2 c. frozen whipped topping,
   thawed

Prepare pudding with milk according to package directions; cool. Pour into pie crust and top with whipped topping. Chill for 3 hours, or until ready to serve. Makes 8 servings.

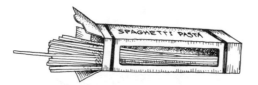

No cake tester or toothpick on hand?
Use a strand of uncooked spaghetti to test cakes!

Short & Sweet Desserts

Ice Cream Sandwich Cake

Mecca McIntyre
Rebecca, GA

Ideal for a reunion dessert...make it the night before if you'd like.

24 ice cream sandwiches
2 12-oz. containers frozen
　whipped topping, thawed

Garnish: caramel ice cream
　topping
Optional: chopped nuts

Layer ice cream sandwiches side-by-side in an ungreased
13"x9 baking pan. Cover with whipped topping; drizzle with caramel
topping. Add nuts, if desired; freeze 2 hours before serving.
Serves 10 to 12.

Fingerprints come off appliances in seconds with a solution of
half vinegar and half water. Apply with a soft towel; wipe dry.

Cherry Pink Salad

Terri Lock
Waverly, MO

*I like to top this salad with colorful jimmies or
sprinkles...my 4 kids love it served this way!*

2 21-oz. cans cherry pie filling
20-oz. can crushed pineapple,
   drained
8-oz. container frozen whipped
   topping, thawed

3 c. mini marshmallows
Optional: chopped nuts

Mix together pie filling and pineapple. Add whipped topping and blend
until pink. Stir in marshmallows and nuts; transfer to serving bowl.
Chill until ready to serve. Makes 8 to 10 servings.

Sometimes glasses that are stacked become stuck together.
Pour cold water in the top glass and dip the bottom glass in
very warm water; gently pull apart.

Short & Sweet Desserts

Speedy Strawberry Shortcake

Nancy Wise
Little Rock, AR

Simple, fresh ingredients make this a real family pleaser!

3/4 c. whipping cream
2 T. powdered sugar
1/2 t. vanilla extract

8 shortbread cookies
16 strawberries, hulled and
quartered

Combine cream, powdered sugar and vanilla in a mixing bowl. Beat with an electric mixer on high speed until light and fluffy. Arrange 2 cookies on each of 4 dessert plates; top with whipped cream mixture and strawberries. Serve immediately. Serves 4.

To remove strawberry stains from clothing, combine
1/2 teaspoon liquid laundry detergent with 1/4 cup each of
white vinegar and cool water. Soak the stain. If the stain
remains, rinse with cool water, apply a few drops of vinegar, and
rinse with water again. Wash again according to clothing label.

No-Flour Peanut Butter Cookies

Barbara Pache
Marshall, WI

Unbelievably good and yes, there's really no flour needed!

1 egg, beaten
1 c. sugar
1 t. baking soda

1 c. crunchy peanut butter
1 t. vanilla extract

Combine all ingredients; roll into about 24 balls. Bake at 350 degrees on a lightly greased baking sheet for 10 to 12 minutes. Makes about 2 dozen.

To remove labels placed on fruit, place a short length of transparent tape over the label and gently peel off. The sticker will come right off with the tape!

Short & Sweet Desserts

Peanut Butter Fudge

Barb Glenn
Mansfield, OH

There's only 2 ingredients in this fudge!

18-oz. jar crunchy or smooth   16-oz. container vanilla frosting
    peanut butter

Combine peanut butter and frosting in a microwave-safe bowl;
cook on high setting for one minute. Stir until blended; spread into a
lightly greased 8"x8" baking pan. Refrigerate until fudge sets up, about
10 minutes. Cut into squares. Makes 3-1/2 dozen pieces.

Wash Grandma's crystal or dishes by hand and always wear
rubber gloves. You'll get a safe grip and they won't slip
out of your hands in the soapy water.

Banana Split Dessert

Tina Wright
Atlanta, GA

Bananas, cherries, pineapple and nuts...this dessert has it all.

14-oz. can sweetened
   condensed milk
12-oz. container frozen whipped
   topping, thawed
21-oz. can cherry pie filling

3 bananas, thickly sliced
8-oz. can crushed pineapple,
   drained
1/2 c. chopped nuts

Combine sweetened condensed milk and whipped topping until well blended. Fold in pie filling, bananas, pineapple and nuts. Refrigerate until ready to serve. Makes 6 to 8 servings.

Cut the top off of a clean plastic milk jug, leaving the handle on...an easy-to-tote cleaning supply holder!

Short & Sweet Desserts

Pears Extraordinaire

Susan Metzger
Washougal, WA

Pears with honey, brown sugar and caramel...oh my!

2 pears, cored, peeled and sliced
1/4 c. apple juice
2 T. cream cheese, softened
2 T. honey
2 t. brown sugar, packed

1/2 t. vanilla extract
4 t. caramel ice cream topping
4 t. chopped pecans
Garnish: 4 T. frozen whipped
   topping, thawed

Arrange pear slices cut-side down in a microwave-safe dish. Drizzle with apple juice. Cover and microwave on high setting for 5 to 7 minutes, or until pears are tender; set aside. Mix together cream cheese, honey, brown sugar and vanilla until creamy and smooth. Arrange pears cut-side up on 4 serving plates. Spoon one-quarter of cream cheese mixture in the center of each pear. Sprinkle one teaspoon pecans over cream cheese mixture and drizzle with one teaspoon caramel ice cream topping. Garnish with whipped topping. Serves 4.

A damp cloth and a little white toothpaste
(not the gel type) will work wonders to remove crayon
marks from the floor or the wall.

Grandma's Pistachio Dessert

Laura Fuller
Fort Wayne, IN

Sure to show up on Sunday dinner tables...it's always expected.

3.4-oz. pkg. instant pistachio
    pudding mix
8-oz. container frozen whipped
    topping, thawed
20-oz. can crushed pineapple

1 c. mini marshmallows
1/2 c. chopped walnuts
1/4 c. maraschino cherries,
    chopped

Blend together pudding mix and whipped topping. Gradually add pineapple with juice. Fold in marshmallows, walnuts and cherries. Refrigerate until ready to serve. Makes 6 to 8 servings.

Use a sugar shaker to save clean up time in the kitchen.
Ideal for dusting cookies and desserts warm from the oven
and no risk of tipping over the sugar bag!

Short & Sweet Desserts

Apple Pie Parfaits

Annette Ingram
Grand Rapids, MI

Top with a sprinkling of chopped walnuts too.

2 21-oz. cans apple pie filling
1 qt. vanilla ice cream
1/2 t. cinnamon

Garnish: frozen whipped
topping, thawed

Pour pie filling into a microwave-safe bowl. Cover and heat on high setting for one to 2 minutes, or until hot. Spoon pie filling into parfait glasses; top with vanilla ice cream. Sprinkle with cinnamon; top with a dollop of whipped topping. Serves 8.

Cinnamon-Blueberry Sauce

Barbara Hess
Boise, ID

Great served over vanilla ice cream or vanilla yogurt.

1/4 c. brown sugar substitute
2 t. cornstarch
2 c. frozen blueberries

1/4 c. water
2 T. lemon or lime juice
2 t. cinnamon

Combine brown sugar substitute and cornstarch in a small saucepan. Add blueberries, water, lemon or lime juice and cinnamon. Bring to a boil over medium heat. Reduce heat and simmer, uncovered, for 5 minutes, stirring frequently. Serves 4.

Super idea! Keep a brand-new shoehorn in the kitchen for lifting muffins out of the muffin tin without tearing them.

Index

Index

Index

We've cooked up a whole collection of Gooseberry Patch® books!

Have a taste for more? Call us toll-free at
1-800-854-6673
We'll send you our latest catalog filled with kitchenware, candles, handmade quilts, gourmet goodies, enamelware, bowls, bubble night lights and our very own line of cookbooks, calendars and organizers!

Phone us:
1·800·854·6673

Fax us:
1·740·363·7225

Visit our website:
www.gooseberrypatch.com

Send us your favorite recipe!

*and the memory that makes it special for you!** If we select your recipe for a brand-new **Gooseberry Patch** cookbook, your name will appear right along with it...and you'll receive a FREE copy of the book! Mail to:

Gooseberry Patch
Attn: Book Dept.
P.O. Box 190
Delaware, OH 43015

*Please include the number of servings and all other necessary information!

U.S. to Canadian recipe equivalents

Volume Measurements

1/4 teaspoon	1 mL
1/2 teaspoon	2 mL
1 teaspoon	5 mL
1 tablespoon = 3 teaspoons	15 mL
2 tablespoons = 1 fluid ounce	30 mL
1/4 cup	60 mL
1/3 cup	75 mL
1/2 cup = 4 fluid ounces	125 mL
1 cup = 8 fluid ounces	250 mL
2 cups = 1 pint =16 fluid ounces	500 mL
4 cups = 1 quart	1 L

Weights

1 ounce	30 g
4 ounces	120 g
8 ounces	225 g
16 ounces = 1 pound	450 g

Oven Temperatures

300° F	150° C
325° F	160° C
350° F	180° C
375° F	190° C
400° F	200° C
450° F	230° C

Baking Pan Sizes

Square

8x8x2 inches	2 L = 20x20x5 cm
9x9x2 inches	2.5 L = 23x23x5 cm

Rectangular

13x9x2 inches	3.5 L = 33x23x5 cm

Loaf

9x5x3 inches	2 L = 23x13x7 cm

Round

8x1-1/2 inches	1.2 L = 20x4 cm
9x1-1/2 inches	1.5 L = 23x4 cm